Sagittarius

23 November – 22 December

First published in Great Britain 2010
by Harlequin Mills & Boon Limited,
Eton House, 18-24 Paradise Road, Richmond, Surrey TW9 1SR

Copyright © Dadhichi Toth 2007, 2008, 2009, 2010 & 2011

ISBN: 978 0 263 87386 3

Typeset at Midland Typesetters Australia

Harlequin Mills & Boon policy is to use papers that are
natural, renewable and recyclable products and made from
wood grown in sustainable forests. The logging and
manufacturing processes conform to the legal environmental
regulations of the country of origin.

Printed and bound in Spain
by Litografia Rosés S.A., Barcelona

About
Dadhichi

Dadhichi is one of Australia's foremost astrologers. He has the ability to draw from complex astrological theory to provide clear, easily understandable advice and insights for people who want to know what their futures might hold.

In the 27 years that Dadhichi has been practising astrology, face reading and other esoteric studies, he has conducted over 9,500 consultations. His clients include celebrities, political and diplomatic figures, and media and corporate identities from all over the world.

Dadhichi's unique blend of astrology and face reading helps people fulfil their true potential. His extensive experience in western astrology is complemented by his research into the theory and practice of eastern systems of astrology.

Dadhichi is a regular columnist for several Australian magazines. He often appears as a guest on leading Australian television and radio networks, where many of his political and world-wide forecasts have proved uncannily accurate.

His websites www.astrology.com.au, www.facereader.com, www.soulconnector.com and www.psychjuice.com attract hundreds of thousands of visitors each month, and offer a wide variety of features, helpful information and services.

Dedicated to The Light of Intuition
Sri V. Krishnaswamy—mentor and friend
With thanks to Julie, Joram, Isaac and Janelle

Welcome from
Dadhichi

Dear Friend,

Welcome to your astrological forecast for 2011! I've spent considerable time preparing these insights for you. My goal is to give you an overview of your sign and I hope you can use my simple suggestions to steer you in the right direction.

I am often asked by my clients to help them understand their true path and what they are supposed to be doing in life. This is a complex task; however, astrology can assist with finding some answers. In this book I attempt to reveal those unique character traits that define who you are. With a greater self-understanding, you can effectively begin *to live who you are* rather than wondering about *what you should do*. Identity is the key!

Knowing when the best opportunities in your life are likely to appear is the other benefit of astrology, based on planetary transits and forecasting. The latter part of the book deals with what is *likely* to happen on a yearly, monthly and daily basis. By coupling this section with the last chapter, an effective planner, you can conduct your business, relationships and personal affairs in ways that yield maximum benefits for you.

Along with your self-knowledge, there are two other key attitudes you must carry with you: *trust* and *courage*. Unless you're prepared to take a gamble in life, earnestly and fearlessly, you'll stay stuck in the same place, never really growing or progressing. At some point you have to take a step forward. When you synchronise yourself with the powerful talents found in your Sun sign, you'll begin to understand what your mission in life will be. This is the true purpose and use of astrology.

So I invite you to gear up for an exciting fifteen months! Don't shrink back from life, even if at times some of the forecasts seem a little daunting. Don't forget that humans are always at their best when the going gets tough. The difficult planetary transits are merely invitations to bring out the best in yourself, while the favourable planetary cycles are seasons for enjoying the benefits that karma has in store for you.

Remain positive, expect the best, and see the beauty in everyone and everything. Remember the words of a great teacher: 'The world is as you see it.' In other words, life will reflect back to you only what you are willing to see.

I trust the coming fifteen months will grant you wonderful success, health, love and happiness. May the light of the Sun, the Moon and all of the stars fill your heart with joy and satisfaction.

Your Astrologer,

Dadhichi Toth

Contents

The Sagittarius Identity 1

    Sagittarius: A Snapshot 3

Star Sign Compatibility 23

2011: The Year Ahead 55

**Your Bonus 2010
Three Month Forecast** 69

    October 2010 71

    November 2010 76

    December 2010 81

2011: Month by Month Predictions 85

    January 2011 87

February 2011 92

March 2011 97

April 2011 102

May 2011 107

June 2011 112

July 2011 117

August 2011 122

September 2011 127

October 2011 132

November 2011 137

December 2011 142

2011: Astronumerology 147

2011: Your Daily Planner 173

SAGITTARIUS

The Sagittarius
Identity

*A failure is a man who has blundered, but is not able
to cash in on the experience.*

— Elbert Hubbard

Sagittarius: A Snapshot

Key Characteristics

Magnanimous, honest, expansive, generous, reckless,
extroverted, proud, larger than life, free

Compatible Star Signs

Aries, Leo, Libra, Aquarius

Key Life Phrase

I expand

Life Goals

To explore the world and grow in understanding

Platinum Assets

Fearlessness, optimism and goodwill

Zodiac Totem

The Centaur

Zodiac Symbol

♐

Zodiac Facts

Ninth sign of the zodiac; mutable, barren, masculine, dry

Element

Fire

Famous Sagittarians

Ludwig van Beethoven, Mark Twain, Ben Stiller,
Bruce Lee, Britney Spears, Walt Disney, Jane Austen,
Tina Turner, Tyra Banks, Brad Pitt, Benjamin Bratt,
Keith Richards, Steven Spielberg, Gianni Versace,
Bette Midler

Sagittarius: Your profile

Sagittarius, the archer, is the ninth sign of the zodiac and a mutable fire sign ruled by jovial Jupiter. Fire can alter substances, and similarly, Sagittarians can transform negative situations into positive ones with their optimism. Obstacles that others see as mountains are just bumps in the road of life to a Sagittarian.

The symbol of Sagittarius is the centaur; half man, half beast. The additional feature of your totem is the bow and arrow that the centaur holds and steadily aims at the wide blue yonder. That's you, Sagittarius, aiming as high as you can to achieve whatever is possible in life.

This star sign has a frank and open nature, bordering on bluntness at times, but it is not because they want to hurt anyone's feelings, simply because they want to get their point across without a lot of window dressing.

Sagittarians can be overconfident, which goes hand in hand with their inbuilt enthusiasm for life and their happy-go-lucky nature. It would be hard to be in the company of a Sagittarian and not be somewhat touched by their views on the world. They are 'can do' types of people, not 'can't do'. Likewise, Sagittarians need positive people around them just as much as they need air to breathe.

Your ruling planet Jupiter is responsible for your luck. But you believe that nothing will go wrong, anyway, and for this reason you are sometimes seen as a bit of a risk taker and will give most things a go, at least once. Adventure should be your middle name and, while family and friends may sometimes hold back and be frightened by your attitude, they can't help being impressed by your willingness to have a go.

A possessive friend or partner will send you running for the hills—and not just for the exercise. Your need to be free is at the centre of your being and, if anyone tries to fence you in or curb your natural enthusiasm for life, they will only see your dust as you race off into the distance to get as far away from them as possible.

Sagittarians are generally physically strong and robust, needing to be this way to handle the million-and-one activities they try to cram into a day. You are energetic, quick to move (although not always gracefully), and have bright, intelli-gent sparkling eyes that often twinkle with good humour. Excess weight can be a problem for a Sagittarian if they are shorter rather than taller in appearance.

This sign of the zodiac has a well-developed sense of social justice and, although pleasure loving, you are also aware of the plight of many people in this world because Jupiter is also the planet of beneficence. Travel will be high on your list of 'must dos' and Sagittarians can often be found exploring countries that are not necessarily standard destinations on tourist maps. You want to develop your sense of spiritual connectedness to people from all over the world, and travel is the most likely way you will do it.

You will spend your whole life expanding your knowledge and the subjects that interest you will be wide and varied. You need to understand how things work, why things happen the way they do, and are forever trying to get to the bottom things and understand why life is the way it is. You will be attracted to people who also thirst for knowledge and understanding.

Personal growth and self-understanding are driving forces for you and gathering interesting facts and figures is part of your search and growth. Your life may seem like one big pilgrimage in your quest for self-knowledge.

Your timing is incredible and somehow you always seem to be in the right place at the right time. It is uncanny how often this happens with friendships, jobs or buying a house, to give a few examples. You also seem to be able to source out those people who can help you achieve your ambitions because you are not afraid to ask questions to achieve your aims.

Jupiter, as your ruler, Sagittarius, is one of the most intuitive planets, and you should always trust your gut feelings when you meet someone new or are faced with a situation you haven't experienced before. Your inbuilt intuition will not let you down.

You can make your home almost anywhere, along the lines of the old saying, 'wherever I lay my hat, that's my home'. It is not unusual for Sagittarians to be world travellers, spending their time living overseas or even having several homes in different countries. Sagittarians are usually planning their next journey before they have even unpacked from the present one.

Usually you are not well domesticated and would rather chat to friends than do a basket of ironing. But, you muddle through, and anyone dropping into your home unannounced will always get a warm welcome.

Three classes of Sagittarius

If you are born between the 23rd of November and the 2nd of December you are a true Sagittarian and will exhibit the traits mentioned in full. Always optimistic and ready for an adventure, life will be full of pleasure and unexpected good fortune.

If your birth date falls between the 3rd and the 12th of December, fiery Mars and Aries as well as Sagittarius rule you. You are a spicier and more hot-tempered class of Sagittarian and are always on the go, but you can also get yourself into hot water with your impulsiveness. Being physical by nature,

7

sports will be an important component of keeping yourself stable and peaceful.

The third group of Sagittarians born between the 13th and 22nd of December are co-ruled by the Sun and Leo. The majestic royal solar energies endow you with an incredibly strong sense of self and also the likelihood of tremendous success, personally and financially. You will also develop a more spiritual attitude as you get older.

Sagittarius role model: Tyra Banks

The Sagittarian spirit of enterprise and independence is seen in model Tyra Banks, as well as her continual drive to reach for greater and more exciting successes. After making it as a model, she successfully produced and hosted reality TV shows and her own talk show, through which she is genuinely trying to help others. Although somewhat outspoken, her motives are pure.

Sagittarius: The light side

You can be down but not necessarily out, Sagittarius. Sometimes life deals you a crummy hand, but with your supreme optimism, it is not long before you bounce back up again. You always try to see the best in a situation, even though sometimes you need to dig deep to find it. But find it you will.

You look for positive outcomes where others give up. But giving up is not in your nature. Your attitude can inspire others, but it also may confuse them because they don't quite understand how you can possibly see good in the bad, and opportunity in a failure.

Although you would prefer to win, winning is not the driving force behind what you do in any games you play. You enjoy the excitement of the sport for the sake of the thrill, not just what is on the score board.

You will have friends from many backgrounds in life and will take in all kinds of people to your home just as you would a stray puppy, while not expecting anything in return for that gesture. You are happy to lend a helping hand to anyone in need, simply because they are in a bit of trouble.

Sagittarius: The shadow side

It is unusual for a Sagittarian to have only one or two people as friends, but anyone who tries to get too familiar with you too quickly, or take advantage of your natural friendliness, will experience the fiery rocket of the Sagittarian temper. You usually fight with words that can be as sharp as darts and just as accurate in hitting their intended targets; but in extreme cases, you may even use your fists.

You may need to listen more to other people's viewpoints before getting up on your soapbox and sprouting about how you see the world. Doing this can be seen as being bombastic or egotistical, when actually all you want to do is to have your say.

Risk and adventure are part of your make-up, but these approaches to life can also lead to such problems as gambling, which impact on your friends and family if you lose a lot of money. You need to be aware of your personal responsibilities before betting any large amount of money.

Staying in one spot doesn't come easily to a Sagittarian, but if you can develop a taste for some quiet times in your life, you will learn to focus on balance rather than constantly seeking the thrills and spills of new experiences.

Sagittarius woman

The loving and compassionate energy of Jupiter is present in the Sagittarian woman and you'll have the most wonderful blend of honesty and kind heartedness. You are the sign of the zodiac that will help those in need, expecting nothing in return, and will probably fall for the odd hard luck story and be taken for a ride. But that won't stop you holding out your helping hand and this is one of the things that your friends most like about you.

Not many people can laugh at themselves, but you, Sagittarius, don't have a problem with this aspect of your nature. You feel that, because you try so many new things, there are bound to be some disasters. But what would life be without these peaks and troughs? It would be a flat line, and that version of boring is not something you even want to know about.

You may be a little blunt and sometimes shoot from the lip (no, I don't mean 'hip'), but this is never meant to hurt anyone. It is just your way of letting people know it's time for them to back off a little, otherwise there will be the old fight or flight response from you if your freedom is threatened in any way.

You have a strong sense of humour that is likely to break out in an instant, sometimes catching others unaware because they may not see the funny side as quickly as you do. And usually you have laughed and moved onto something else before they have even understood what the joke is all about, due to your intelligence and quick-wittedness.

If your integrity is questioned you can become quite angry in a millisecond, and this is where the fire in your Sagittarian sign really flares up. You don't like being intimidated; however, in your desire to be right you can sometimes be a little over-powering with your high level of self-confidence. This can be daunting when people meet you for the first time, but if the friendship endures, they will understand that this is one of your strong traits and they can rely on you to stand by them if and when they need it.

Sagittarian women don't play games as far as the way they dress or act. What you see is what you get, and this can make other women in your company feel uncomfortable because, in comparison, your approach may highlight their pretentiousness. You can spot a phoney at fifty paces and don't waste your time trying to nurture a friendship with these people or bothering to admit them into your circle of acquaintances.

You will have a few close friends and some of them may feel that you are arrogant or egotistical, but this is because you are quite happy being who you are and don't try to hide it. If other people can't deal with your rather forthright personality, then you feel it is their loss, not yours, and they will probably move on. So be it.

You can be a risk taker and other females may think this is either complete madness or showing off, but this may not be so. The world is there for the taking in your view and, if others want to sit back quietly and watch the weeds grow, then that is their choice, but definitely not yours. You are not very worried about what people think of you and understand that the average person doesn't have the same degree of energy and optimism as you do.

Sagittarius man

The Sagittarian male is a positive thinker, in possession of abundant energy, and has a very gregarious humour. Combine all this with your optimism and you will stop at nothing to achieve satisfaction in all areas of your life. You are a man on the go, always searching for new mountains to climb and horizons to reach and, with your energy levels, you usually leave friends and colleagues behind in the dust.

Your personality is warm and vital because you are a fire sign. With your self-confidence, you attract people to you in droves. You are a great storyteller but are prone to exaggeration and often forget a punch line when telling a joke, but this doesn't daunt you at all. It is just part of life's big tapestry and is who you are. Take it or leave it.

You like people but need to monitor how far they can be pushed with your grand ideas and never-ending plans for new adventures. You treat all people equally and can accommodate various views, philosophies and people from different cultures and backgrounds. It is all interesting to you because you are the eternal scholar, wanting to learn as much as you can. Travel is one of the ways you can do this. It would be a dream job if you could combine your profession with travel.

Sagittarians are competitive and sport is one area in which they usually appear in the forefront. Sports such as tennis, cricket, golf, football, or even air or water sports grab you—and the more spirited, the better—because you thrive on pushing yourself to the limit.

It is not only in sport that you are competitive, for it also flows over into your professional life, too. With your people skills, storytelling abilities and self-confidence, your audience will be captivated. You have a great way of communicating ideas and are probably one of the more honest signs of the zodiac. However, remember to take some honey with you to sweeten your rather blunt honesty when you want to cut straight to the crux of any matter. Those who are more sensitive can feel rather wounded if they are not resilient.

Sagittarian males have a good memory for facts and figures; but in their whirlwind of daily life they can be forgetful about simple things like where they left their car keys. You will bring great joy to your family and make a very good role model for your children. Some Sagittarian men never grow up themselves and always remain big kids at heart.

You like to take a punt now and again but be aware that it is in your nature to take risks. Do not alienate friends or family by using, and possibly losing, money that is earmarked for something else. Gambling can become an addiction in your star sign, so you need to understand the potential ramifications of this activity.

Sagittarius child

Love is essential to all children, but never more so than to the young Sagittarian. However, it must be delivered in a certain way. Leave any possessiveness and smother love at the door because your Sagittarian child will react much better to encouragement and showing your pleasure in simply having them in your life.

A Sagittarian child will hide their hurts, disappointments and sorrows behind a spirited belief that everything will get better eventually. They can be seen as the clown who laughs while their heart is breaking. These restless, freedom-loving children need lots of room to play and tend to get more bumps and bruises than others because they are rarely still and always off on some adventure, somewhere, whether real or imaginary.

The Sagittarian child will be popular at school because they are kind, generous and will look after the underdog, which is their sense of social justice coming to the fore. They are usually intelligent, quick-witted and catch on before many of their peers. The faster they learn the lessons for the day, the sooner they can head off on some exploit or another to learn new things.

From the first day they are on this earth they are eager to get going and are restless little individuals, but they do need a disciplined regime to help them get ready for life as a whole. They need mental stimulation but also the opportunity to explore many hobbies and sports until they settle on what works for them.

The Sagittarian child is competitive and can be a little bossy with their peers, so they need to be trained from an early age in the process of give and take. This will stand them in good stead as they grow up on their way to becoming balanced and self-fulfilled adults.

Because Sagittarians have the notion of 'bigger, biggest, best' in their attitudes, this can also flow over into their food habits, which could mean weight gain problems if their diet is unbalanced and too rich in sweets. Although they need lots of energy to get through their days, watch their diets and teach them as they grow older how to eat what's best for them.

Sagittarian children are constantly asking questions. As they get older they will not see any reason why they shouldn't question adult views and what they see as hypocrisy in some opinions. The best thing that parents of a Sagittarian child can do is be totally honest with them.

Romance, love and marriage

To Sagittarius, love is a romantic adventure to be enjoyed and explored without feeling tied down, but you also need to feel secure in that love. You have no hesitation in sharing your feelings, and like your partner to stimulate and amuse you as well as enjoy your company. You love to touch and cuddle, and a big, warm hug is your form of security blanket that makes you feel wanted.

Although some Sagittarians may indulge in the occasional affair, in these instances their attraction will be more about the excitement rather than a true romance. You need a solid intellectual compatibility to take any relationship to the next level and feel contentment in the long-term. The partnership may not survive if the other person is possessive or jealous of you and, if this is the case, it's possible you could just pack up and move on without so much as a backward glance. It will be a smart partner who realises early on in the relationship that freedom means everything to a Sagittarian.

The female Sagittarian loves to be loved for her outspoken charm; her words and actions show what she is thinking and feeling. She will want a partner who does not play silly games because she herself is not coy and evasive, and her partner must always *ask* her to do something, never *tell* her.

The male Sagittarian would like a partner who will not try to control him, check up on him or falsely accuse him of looking elsewhere. This would be the end of the relationship once the trust has gone.

People are naturally attracted to you, Sagittarius, because you are open, honest and don't hide behind a carefully crafted mask. You are spontaneous and optimistic that life will provide you with what you need when you need it, and you see no reason to exclude love from this equation.

It might take quite a few relationships on several different levels before you find the one you are looking for who can step up to the challenge of being with you, romantically speaking.

Venus the planet of love has a strong influence on the lives of Sagittarians and dominates your zone of friendships and social life. You want someone with a sense of elegance and style, who can step up to the plate and is able to express a classy side of life.

You have a very amorous nature at times but need to be mindful that your search for passion can over-stimulate you to such an extent that you may miss out on emotional satisfaction. And, if your partner does not come up to par as far as intellectual prowess is concerned, you might need to look a bit deeper into their character before you write them off. Sometimes there are other traits in your partner that can contribute to your long-term satisfaction in a relationship.

When looking for a partner it is important that their role is not just sexual but that they support you in whatever you choose to achieve in life. You have a great deal of enthusiasm; therefore, if your partner is on your team when you are setting your goals, you must also support them in return.

With your yen for travel you may even meet someone on one of your trips who comes from another culture or country. This will provide you with another learning experience if they have the personal qualities you are looking for.

Fire signs are creative and therefore your partner needs to have a certain amount of creativity or you will probably lose interest in them fairly quickly, especially if the bedroom activity becomes dull and boring. Sport and play are as essential for you in love as they are in life and those partners born under the star signs of Gemini, Libra and Aquarius will give you the mental stimulation that you need.

Once you settle down and marry, you will give 100 per cent commitment of your mind and heart and this will be a wonderful platform to start raising a family. You also need an active domestic life, and social encounters that are filled with fun and adventure to make your marriage satisfying in the long-term.

Health, wellbeing and diet

You are a fairly robust sign, Sagittarius, and generally have a strong body and good health. Even though Jupiter is your ruling planet and ensures you a long life, you must learn to curb your excessive traits such as eating too much of the wrong foods.

Confining you to bed with an illness is almost like being sent to a torture chamber for you because it restricts your movements. However, the other side of the coin is that you could use this time resting to plan your upcoming adventure or dream a little about what's next on the Sagittarian calendar.

Constitutionally you are quite strong but your weak points could benefit from regular massages and yoga to help keep your thighs, hips, pelvis and lower back in tip-top condition. Your neck and upper shoulders could also give you a bit of trouble later in life.

Your optimistic mental attitude will help you overcome most illnesses. Diseases that attack Sagittarians usually concern the hips and legs; for example, problems that arise from falling over or colliding with something because you are always on the go. You are generally fond of animals so you need to be wary of diseases that are transmissible.

Being overweight can be a problem for you if your food intake and exercise output is not finely balanced. Your diet should have plenty of vegetables, lentils, broccoli, olives and the greener leafy vegetables so that you get all the nutrients needed for your fast-paced lifestyle.

Meat, if you must eat it, should be low fat and trimmed. It is better if you can eat more white meat than red, and lots of fish but preferably not the fatty kind. Stay away from excessively fatty processed foods like salami because Jupiter regulates the liver and this indicates that some of you may have a problem processing these highly refined foods.

Sagittarians do not have a lot of willpower when it comes to rich food and fine dining, but if you eat smaller meals and exercise regularly, then these actions will help solve any problems for you.

Later in the day, your metabolism slows down, making you less able to burn off any high-calorie foods. Therefore it is better if you eat less as the day goes on, so that your biggest meal of the day is breakfast, which will kick-start you and get you on the move.

Work

Virgo rules your zone of employment and has much to do with your skills in fine detail work as well as your big picture views. Some Sagittarians may not seem all that driven or ambitious because of their carefree and easygoing nature; whereas in fact, many hardworking and successful individuals have been born under this sign.

Your enthusiasm for the work at hand, combined with your skills and inability to take no for an answer, makes you an employee who gets the job done. Professions such as teaching and corporate or executive training are just made for you and, with Jupiter being your ruling planet, you also have the ability to work in banking, finance, law, foreign relations or the import–export industry, where travel and culture will create added appeals for you.

If someone chooses to partner a Sagittarian in business, they can expect to find honesty and plenty of creative ideas in you. It will work even better if they allow you independence and freedom within it. Even in the most routine of jobs you will seek out challenges so that you don't get tired and bored.

Sagittarians are big-picture people. They can be hard to tie down when asked for details on the job they are doing because they prefer to get on with doing it at their own speed, which is usually flat out!

Key to karma, spirituality and emotional balance

Your element is that of fire, Sagittarius, and your key words are 'I expand'. However, you must learn to balance the need for expansion with some practical constraints so you don't burn out.

By all means set your goals—and there will probably be many of them—but remember that you are only human and must stay within your learned limits and get plenty of rest to begin another day tomorrow at your usual breakneck speed.

Adequate exercise, healthy living and good food will keep you well into old age because Jupiter, your ruling planet, gives you a long life. It is up to you to look after what you have been fortunate enough to be given—a healthy, robust body and an inquisitive mind.

You were headstrong in your past life and your ego was a little too powerful, so this time around you will be learning the lesson of humility.

Your lucky days

Your luckiest days are Mondays, Tuesdays, Thursdays and Sundays.

Your lucky numbers

Remember that the forecasts given later in the book will help you optimise your chances of winning. Your lucky numbers are:

1, 10, 19, 28, 37, 46

3, 12, 21, 30, 39, 48

9, 18, 27, 36, 45, 54

Your destiny years

Your most important years are 3, 12, 21, 30, 39, 48, 57, 66, 75 and 84.

Star Sign Compatibility

You must look into other people as well as at them.

—Lord Chesterfield

Romantic compatibility

How compatible are you with your current partner, lover or friend? Did you know that astrology can reveal a whole new level of understanding between people simply by looking at their star sign and that of their partner? In this chapter I'd like to share some special insights that will help you better appreciate your strengths and challenges using Sun sign compatibility.

The Sun reflects your drive, willpower and personality. The essential qualities of two star signs blend like two pure colours, producing an entirely new colour. Relationships, similarly, produce their own emotional colours when two people interact. The following is a general guide to your romantic prospects with others and how, by knowing the astrological 'colour' of each other, the art of love can help you create a masterpiece.

When reading the following I ask you to remember that no two star signs are ever *totally* incompatible. With effort and compromise, even the most 'difficult' astrological matches can work. Don't close your mind to the full range of life's possibilities! Learning about each other and ourselves is the most important facet of astrology.

Each star sign combination is followed by the elements of those star signs and the results of their combining. For instance, Aries is a fire sign and Aquarius is an air sign, and this combination produces a lot of 'hot air'. Air feeds fire and fire warms air. In fact, fire requires air. However, not all air and fire combinations work. I have included information about the different birth periods within each star sign and this will throw even more light on your prospects for a fulfilling love life with any star sign you choose.

Good luck in your search for love, and may the stars shine upon you in 2011!

Compatibility quick-reference guide

Each of the twelve star signs has a greater or lesser affinity with one another. The quick-reference guide will show you who's hot and who's not so hot as far as your relationships are concerned.

SAGITTARIUS + ARIES
Fire + Fire = Explosion

This is one of the best matches for you, astrologically speaking, Sagittarius. This blend of fire plus fire can only lead to one hot relationship, and it wouldn't surprise me to see you having a thrill a minute! This attraction is due to the fact that you were both born under the same element, and when these two meet, it is usually love at first sight.

There would not be many other signs who could keep up with you, Sagittarius, but generally Aries will give you a good run for your money. They are

Quick-reference guide: Horoscope compatibility between signs (percentage)

	Aries	Taurus	Gemini	Cancer	Leo	Virgo	Libra	Scorpio	Sagittarius	Capricorn	Aquarius	Pisces
Aries	60	65	65	65	90	45	70	80	90	50	55	65
Taurus	60	70	70	80	70	90	75	85	50	95	80	85
Gemini	70	70	75	60	80	75	90	60	75	50	90	50
Cancer	65	80	60	75	70	75	60	95	55	45	70	90
Leo	90	70	80	70	85	75	65	75	95	45	70	75
Virgo	45	90	75	75	75	70	80	85	70	95	50	70
Libra	70	75	90	60	65	80	80	85	80	85	95	50
Scorpio	80	85	60	95	75	85	85	90	85	65	60	95
Sagittarius	90	50	75	55	95	70	80	85	85	55	60	75
Capricorn	50	95	50	45	45	95	85	65	55	85	70	85
Aquarius	55	80	90	70	70	50	95	60	60	70	80	55
Pisces	65	85	50	90	75	70	50	95	75	85	55	80

also one of the few star signs who can cop it on the chin when you deliver one of your verbal punches and they won't hold a grudge.

You understand each other very well and this is because your ruling planets are responsive to each other. Likewise, you have a sense that somehow your qualities are reflected in the other. Aries people are almost as spontaneous as you are and can also be unpredictable, giving you the feeling, Sagittarius, that they will be able to meet any of your needs for adventure in the future.

You are a great combination and can do well in a business or creative venture. You, Sagittarius, have vision, and Aries has drive. They will inspire you and work well with you. Because you have karmic connections, you could expect some good luck to eventuate from a meeting that will feel as though it was predestined.

Aries can provoke you into discussions that can become argumentative, but they are usually short lived. From some of these thought-provoking verbal jousts may come some of your best ideas, especially where business or travel is concerned.

You will love to go on exotic journeys together and your physical abilities are a great match, both of you having large stores of vitality and energy.

Your sexual appetites border on the extreme and you are well suited to each other in the bedroom. You both love the 'art' of love and need it to be physical and engaging, with plenty of passionate times where you can push each other to the limits. There may even be a competitive aspect to your lovemaking.

Is passion what you want? Then team up with an Aries born between the 21st and the 30th of March, especially if you happen to be born between the 2nd and the 11th of December. Watch the sparks fly with this match!

If you're a Sagittarian your best match with an Aries will be with those born between the 31st of March and the 10th of April. You have the uncanny ability to be able to tune into each other's needs at just the right time.

If it's a long-term and stable romantic partnership that you're looking for, choose an Aries born between the 11th and the 20th of April. They are not quite as active as the typical Aries but you will have plenty of exciting social connections with them and, although they will ground you, they won't make you feel that life has to be lived in Dullsville.

SAGITTARIUS + TAURUS
Fire + Earth = Lava

You are a freedom lover, Sagittarius, whereas Taurus is very different. They are practical, down-to-earth and may like to live their lives in what you would call a compartmentalised cell. They are concerned with 'things' of this world, what they can touch and feel, and like to lead a predictable lifestyle. You, on the other hand, will take off in a minute if the lure of adventure proves too strong, leaving any structured routine behind covered in your dust.

With your love of exploring the unknown, living life on the edge and wanting to be able to maintain your freedom, you may make Taurus feel unsettled and perhaps not reassure them as much as they would like. You tend to take life as it comes and Taurus may see your adventurous lifestyle as threatening to the security that they need. But you have practical commonsense and so need to let Taurus know that you do indeed have a balanced view towards both aspects of life, which will go a long way in easing their concerns.

Having a fabulous social life will be important to both of you, but while you have a more direct and lively sort of temperament, Taurus is more cautious in their choice of friends and your rather upfront manner may grate on them. Over time you could feel that they are just a little too stuck in their ways and quite inflexible in their opinions. You don't want to get stuck in a rut, just as they don't want to move ahead as creatively or spontaneously as you do.

To make a relationship work between these two star signs there would need to be quite a lot of adjustment. One of your finer points, Sagittarius, is your great ability to change and adapt to different circumstances. Taurus is less able to do this and could become confused when they witness your chameleon transitions. Think the words 'compromise' and 'adaptability' for the sake of this combination, especially where money issues are concerned.

You need to understand that Taurus does not have the zodiac sign of the bull for nothing. They are stubborn and no amount of pushing and shoving will make them change their mind or their ways, irrespective of how rational your ideas may be.

The sexual side of this match doesn't look so dire, however, and a good relationship can be developed. Even though your ruling planets are not particularly friendly, they do provide you with a wealth of sensitivity and caring. If Taurus is able to pare off the layers of the Sagittarian bravado, they'll find a deeper and more compassionate side to you that may surprise them.

Those Taureans born between the 21st and the 29th of April are strongly ruled by Venus and may not be that compatible with you. They are slow, deliberate and could frustrate you, even to the point of poor health.

Your best match would be with a Taurean born between the 30th of April and the 10th of May. They will at least give you the mental stimulation you need to take this relationship to a deeper level.

Money could be the making or breaking of a relationship with those born between the 11th and the 21st of May, because they are the most practical of the Taureans.

SAGITTARIUS + GEMINI
Fire + Air = Hot Air

Here we have a very intriguing combination because Gemini is your opposite zodiac sign. Opposites attract, or so the saying goes, but this match depends on how you want to approach it. When fiery star signs come together with those of air, a very 'combustible' situation is created, which is what the match of Sagittarius and Gemini could be.

Your similarities are that you are both mutable in nature, which means you can expect considerable change and variety in your lives. There will be continual movement and this is vital for a healthy intellectual and emotional environment for both of you. There will be diversity and plenty of mental and physical stimulation, which will appeal to the core of your mutual satisfaction.

An area of interest where you may meet is travel. This suits both of you and jet setting around the globe lets you engage in the cultural and philosophical studies you love while giving Gemini the social interaction they need. Travel is a perfect meeting point for you and it could even mean working or living overseas due to your strong desire for cultural variety as well.

There is good energy between you and your warm and engaging personality will stimulate Gemini, intellectually and in communications. This will provide a lively exchange of verbal, sensual and emotional energy between you, with lots of excitement thrown in for good measure.

It is highly likely that, being opposite signs of the zodiac, your paths will cross at some point in your lives and this will very possibly trigger your romantic and sexual feelings for each other. Air and fire are a natural combination and you will each warm the other, accentuate each other's qualities, allowing for many sensual and emotional exchanges.

If you team up with a Gemini born between the 22nd of May and the 1st of June, you will feel an immediate attraction on every level with this group. This is a great mix of energies and you can fulfil your desires with them. There seems to be an excellent synchronicity, both socially and domestically, between you.

Geminis born between the 2nd and the 12th of June will confuse you. At times you'll feel drawn to them as a friend, but at other times you'll want a more intimate relationship. It's not a bad idea to develop a friendship with them first before tying yourself down emotionally or sexually. In some cases, this group of Geminis can remain your friend for a long time, so before you take the relationship to the next level, make sure you understand what it is you're getting yourself into.

You will like the buzz that comes with Geminis born between the 13th and the 21st of June. This group has great mental agility, clever humour and think they are able to do a dozen things at once—a bit like you, don't you think, Sagittarius? These Geminis have a tendency to take on too much at once, even though they are the consummate multi-taskers of the zodiac. This relationship could take off like a rocket, but also like a rocket, it may burn out quickly and fall to earth.

SAGITTARIUS + CANCER
Fire + Water = Steam

Here we have two diametrically opposed star signs, Sagittarius and Cancer. You are larger than life, outgoing and adventurous, and may at first seem rather overwhelming to the quiet, sensitive and soft Cancer. However, there is still a unique kind of attraction between your star signs, given that your ruling planet, Jupiter, and theirs, the Moon, are friendly in the planetary portfolio.

You are honest to the point of bluntness and at times insensitively so. Although Cancer will appreciate your straightforward and happy manner, they are extremely thin-skinned individuals who will take your brutally honest statements to heart but won't let you know you have upset their feelings.

This may mean that, as they hide their hurt from you, you will continue to interact with them on exactly the same level without ever knowing how they truly feel. You will need to develop sensitivity to their body language to try to find out what is going on in their hearts and minds.

While Cancer is busy hiding their feelings from you, they won't be able to do it for too long, though. At some point, the burning heat of the fiery Sagittarius will bring the usually cool waters of Cancer to the boil, so there could be a few showdowns in this combination.

Cancer is a sexual zodiac sign to you, so there is hope for a hot affair. But it could be fleeting because there are many basic differences between your temperaments. How much energy the two of you are prepared to give to this relationship will determine how long it lasts.

Cancer is a domestic sign, naturally attracted to family and home life, and they will want to know that you too want to have a family and have a genuine desire to support them in that goal.

Cancers born between the 22nd of June and the 3rd of July are hypersensitive and you may need to adjust yourself to this fact and tone down your extravagant gestures because you could unsettle them. You will also need to be more in tune with their feelings because of their increased sensitivity, seeing as it is one of their key personality traits.

A match with Cancers born between the 4th and the 13th of July should be approached slowly before committing yourself to them. There are things that could make this relationship difficult for you in both the long- and short-term, especially to do with issues concerning their individual character, family history and even cultural and philosophical viewpoints. Look carefully at these important issues before signing along the dotted line with this group.

You will feel more comfortable with, and drawn to, Cancers born between the 14th and the 23rd of

July, because they have some of the Jupiter influence that controls your life, too. You resonate well together and can have a happy life if you choose to settle down with them.

If you want to get close to your Cancer partner, quiet cosy nights by the fire will do it. If you feel this match has prospects, don't close your mind to the fact that they may need more tender loving care than other signs of the zodiac.

SAGITTARIUS + LEO
Fire + Fire = Explosion

The combination of Sagittarius and Leo would be hard to beat for compatibility, because you both radiate warmth, power and beauty, which are reflected in the open honesty of your relationship. You are both upfront sort of people, and Leo is one of the few signs of the zodiac that can actually handle your blunt approach and even thrive on it as well. You mirror each other's enthusiasm for life and enjoy what the other has to offer.

You are able to take Leo by the hand, inspire them to travel and enjoy the exploration and discovery of the world. A wonderful time you will have doing so, too.

Because you are so honest, Sagittarius, you sometimes forget that others can't deal with the truth as easily as you can, and you may hurt Leo, who won't forget all that easily. The lion, after all, is king of the jungle and a very proud individual.

Leo will need to learn how to listen to what you have to say without reacting too strongly, to understand that your honesty isn't meant to be cruel, but is rather an attempt to help and improve them. You, however, must understand that a Leo needs to feel they are the masterful one for the most part, which is the nature of their totem, the lion.

Leo, being a Sun sign, has an enthusiastic and energetic approach to life and if you are a typical Sagittarian you will be far more easygoing than your Leo partner. You will understand their needs and bring out the better side of their natures.

You are both fresh and spontaneous in your love life and, because there's a creative spark in your sexual relationship, your physical connection should be loving and very invigorating. This is one of the better sexual combinations of the zodiac and your Leo partner's intuitive understanding of you will bridge the gaps of any differences.

If you team up with a Leo born between the 24th of July and the 4th of August, you can expect a wonderful destiny because the Sun and Leo rule your higher learning and you'll have many flashes of insight about yourself in this combination. This match will also provide you with a tremendous amount of spiritual growth as well.

Meeting a Leo born between the 5th and the 14th of August could be like finding the other half of yourself and in this sense could even be a little unsettling for you. You are so similar in character; love to travel, have enormous optimism, and are generally curious about the world around you. Your discussions will be inspirational.

If it is more a love affair you are searching for, go for a Leo born between the 15th and the 23rd of August because their additional rulership of Mars and Aries promises plenty of passion and sexual satisfaction. Both of you have strong vitality and it is just as well because you will need a little extra fuel with these Leos to keep up with their demands.

SAGITTARIUS + VIRGO
Fire + Earth = Lava

Virgo may be a challenge for you, Sagittarius, given that they are so concerned with handling the minute details and more fiddly aspects of life, which is very much in contrast to your way of doing things. However, this isn't saying your combination can't be successful. You may, in fact, balance each other out quite nicely, especially if you learn to accept each other's views and not get too precious about your own opinions.

It's not so much that you don't like to see things done correctly; it's more to do with your way of thinking. Virgo is (in your opinion) far too preoccupied with perfection and you find this hard to come to terms with because it is not high on your list of priorities. In this case, you may have to be the one who has to adjust if this relationship is to work. While Virgo is busily looking at the myriad of tiny details on the underside of a leaf, you are off on an adventure tramping through the forest at breakneck speed.

If Virgo could just learn to let go of their criticism of every little thing and look at the outcome rather than the process, and you, Sagittarius, give a little more thought to the process rather than the outcome, it could be worth it. Although these adjustments would be equally difficult, with the combined influence of your star signs, the result could be a load of intellectual stimulation that appeals to both of you.

Virgo is the sign of the virgin; but that doesn't mean sex is off the menu, just that there's a basic difference in your attitudes towards love-making, and this is another area where you may need to work harder to develop harmony in your romance.

In the bedroom Virgo is reserved and you like to experiment. So if your sexual connection is going to work, Virgo will need to learn how to put their mind to sleep and enjoy the moment for what it is. If they can do that, things will go very well for this partnership.

It is unlikely that you would be attracted to Virgos born between the 24th of August and the 2nd of September because, astrologically speaking, there isn't a great deal of magnetism between you. The most successful link for this combination would be a professional one and your initial meeting may even be through a work situation. This could lead to a greater interest in each other and maybe set the stage for a romantic involvement further down the track.

Virgos born between the 3rd and the 12th of September will be hard work for you. They are less active than you would like a partner to be but are probably more intellectually orientated. However, they will help you focus your energy and can even assist you in achieving your long-term objectives. There may be some merit to a relationship with these individuals and perhaps you will gain much more than you first thought possible with them.

The group of Virgos born between the 13th and the 23rd of September will probably grate on your nerves. You won't see eye to eye on the details of their daily routine and will need ample time to figure out how their minds work. These are dissimilarities that could be overcome, but it is probably best simply to avoid this group.

SAGITTARIUS + LIBRA
Fire + Air = Hot Air

There is an immediate sense of comfort, ease of communication and general wellbeing when you and Libra connect. This is based primarily on the compatibility of the elements that rule both of you. Sagittarius having fire as its element, and Libra having air, indicates that the flames of your Sagittarian fire will burn brightly in the company of your Libran counterpart.

Other similarities between your signs are that you both love diversity, change and investigating the world and the people with whom you come into contact. Because of this you'll be able to give Libra the excitement and variety they thrive on. This is particularly so when it comes to people, because people are very important to Libra. Being with friends is important to both of you. Libra and Sagittarius are very social star signs and this kind of interaction will take up a large part of your lives.

Librans also make great friends to Sagittarians and support them in all of their endeavours. They can bring out the better qualities of your character as well. There can be good financial understanding between these two star signs that can lead to the betterment of your lifestyles.

With both Libra and Sagittarius enjoying the great outdoors, it is possible that you might actually meet at a vacation spot, or travelling in another country. You are both interested in people of other cultures and the human psyche in general, so you will be out and about studying the world around you. There will be a lot of dynamic activity and movement in your relationship. If you choose a Libran as your partner you will continually be on the go and there will never be a dull moment.

The romantic side of your relationship is a most interesting one. If Libra can recover from the initial shock/horror of your in-your-face attitude, Sagittarius, you'll both start enjoying your intimate moments together. Your romance is always based on straight-forward honesty and balance. You are open towards and share your deepest feelings with each other, and this transparency is the basis for long-lasting relationships and a great omen for your own success.

You'll feel relaxed and, the more you get to know each other, the closer you will become. This includes your sexual compatibility as well. Don't push Libra too far, though, because they are sensitive and don't like being taken beyond the limits of good taste. Once you get to know each other better, your satisfaction will intensify over time.

Librans born between the 24th of September and the 3rd of October are probably a little too fickle for your liking, even though you see much of your own independence in them.

Those Librans born between the 4th and the 13th of October promise some exciting times. Things may get a little zany when the two of you team up. Expect the unexpected!

There are incredibly good opportunities for marriage with Librans born between the 14th and the 23rd of October. With the influence of Gemini and Mercury upon them, which rules your marriage sector, you will be destined for good times with them.

SAGITTARIUS + SCORPIO
Fire + Water = Steam

There is a definite plus in teaming up with a Scorpio because your ruling planets are quite friendly and therefore this is always a good foundation for a promising relationship. When in concert, the co-ruler of Scorpio, Mars, and your own ruler, Jupiter, produce big thinking and far-sightedness, so this will infuse your relationship with the same qualities. You can have immense success together by following your dreams.

You can also be terrific mates because you are both full of optimism, have a positive view of life and feel that nothing is impossible once you put your hearts and minds together. Your outgoing and daring attitude could make Scorpio a little wary at first, but this won't last long. Your Sagittarian warmth will melt the icy core of your Scorpio partner, and then watch the steam rise! Just remember that Scorpio is a serious sign and needs time to warm up to an idea, but this relationship can work if you show respect for this difference.

You'll soon learn that Scorpio can provide you with a deep, meaningful and sexual relationship if you draw them out of their shell and show them how to express their emotions. However, it would be wise to stick to some basic emotional ground rules if you don't want this partnership to burn out. Once Scorpios dedicate themselves to the partner of their choice they will open up and are even quite humorous in many respects, wanting to express their emotions with full intensity.

Once Scorpio learns how to relax they will slowly but surely start to enjoy the lighter and more optimistic side of life with you. They tend to hold grudges and find it hard at times to let go of the past, but with you by their side, it will be so much easier for them. You, Sagittarius, usually have your eyes focused on the horizon, which is not behind but in front of you.

Your love of travel is such a big part of your life. You will be able to open Scorpio's eyes to the great adventures out there and give them a taste of the freedom and variety in the big wide, wonderful world. You will see a whole new side to them if you encourage them to share this part of your being.

Scorpios born between the 24th of October and the 2nd of November are well suited to Sagittarians born between the 2nd of December and the 11th of December. This combination is really fiery and passionate and probably one of the best matches between your two star signs.

Your most formidable partners will be those born between the 3rd and the 12th of November. This is a great partnership. Jupiter and Neptune ruling these individuals means they are not only creative and spiritual but also very compassionate and loving as well. This could be a very successful union.

Scorpios born between the 13th of November and the 22nd of November will pretend to be subservient but will flash you an opposite side if you try to boss them around or arouse their vindictiveness. Don't take anything for granted with this group.

SAGITTARIUS + SAGITTARIUS
Fire + Fire = Explosion

There are only two outcomes for this combination—success or failure. Because you are both fire signs born under the same sign of Sagittarius, you have similar thoughts and patterns of behaviour that need to be closely monitored if you want this relationship to work.

There are strong emotional energies at play in this combination and you both must bring in a measure of control over this aspect of the relationship so that it can be propelled forward rather than being bogged down in vying for domination by one or the other of you. If you join forces with another Sagittarian, you'll probably promise each other not to let the grass grow under your feet because you both value your freedom so much. Freedom is your common thread and therefore your common enemy, but luckily you'll both understand this need in the other and respect it.

You have mutual interests such as philosophy, travel, adventure, sport and anything else that keeps you intellectually and physically mobile. You are always on the go, heading for the next horizon, setting your sights on the next objective, but this could have the effect of you failing to secure a solid foundation for your relationship. This may be where you need to define where freedom ends and commitment begins. Balance your need for variety with a sense of security for a well-grounded and successful relationship.

Your social life will be lots of fun because you are an exciting combination as far as entertaining, wining and dining are concerned. Sagittarians are fiercely competitive, though, so you could end up trying to outdo each other in social situations; but if you must do so, keep it friendly. On the other hand, that competitive streak will come in very handy where sport is concerned.

You are both honest, some may say brutally so on occasion, but there will never be anything hidden between you. Neither of you pull any punches and you'll soon learn that if you want to dish it out, you'll have to take it, too.

Generally you will match well with any Sagittarian, but even more so with those born between the 23rd of November and the 1st of December. They will offer you a ton of variety, love and confidence that you can make a go of things together. You'll have a very social life, filled with friends, and be very supportive of each other. Love will come naturally to the two of you.

Sagittarians born between the 2nd of December and the 11th of December are strongly influenced by Mars, so their physical appetites are very strong. No couch potatoes to be found in this group! They are right into sports and other physical activities and this will be good for you by improving your health.

There is a strong Leo tinge to the group born between the 12th and the 22nd of December. You may be attracted to their bright aura, but they are proud and inflexible in their attitudes, so how you deal with all that will determine the long-term viability of this match. Once you've developed an additional dose of humility, this relationship might have a good chance of working.

SAGITTARIUS + CAPRICORN
Fire + Earth = Lava

You, Sagittarius, have an outgoing temperament, are open, optimistic and straightforward, and have a tendency to take things as they come, no matter what. You have a belief that life is going to work out for the best, even when the most difficult situations present themselves, but you trust you will land firmly on your own two feet.

Capricorn on the other hand tends to hope for the best, but expects the worst, which is diametrically opposed to your view on life and without even a shred of your optimism. Capricorn is regarded as a cold, constricted and inward-looking sign, conservative and a bit uptight. You will need to give Capricorn time to become relaxed with you, but they may at first feel overpowered by your sunny disposition and may even see their own character wanting when compared to yours. However, don't dismiss Capricorn as a probable partner.

Your primary role with Capricorn may be to try to raise their expectations, to increase their optimism to somewhere near the level of your own. However, you may find that, if neither of you is prepared to move towards the middle of the differences in your outlooks, there would seem to be little reason for staying together in a relationship such as this.

You are adventurous and love your freedom, so sport or anything to do with the outdoors might be a mutual meeting ground for you with Capricorn. Although they are not naturally drawn into these sorts of outdoor, high-level and competitive activities, some gentle nudging might help them to come out of their shells.

If you are able to draw them out to share in your love of the outdoors, they might warm to your outgoing ways and join in your escapades. They may at first be cautious, but if you do team up with a Capricorn you will need to take into account the ambitious and practical side of their characters.

The sexual chemistry between you may not be as hot and passionate as you'd like at first, but if you take your time they will eventually satisfy you. Capricorn is actually warmer and more loving than people give them credit for and persistence usually pays off for a Sagittarius.

If you are with a Capricorn born between the 23rd of December and the 1st of January, you're not too likely to experience hot passion in the early days. They are earthy types who need time and persuasion to come around to your way of thinking, but your warmth and passion will win the day.

Capricorns born between the 2nd of January and the 10th of January are far more emotional and sensual than those born in the previous group, but you may need to dig a little deeper below the surface to bring out this trait in them. There is a certain attractiveness in these people to which you are drawn.

The group born between the 11th and the 20th of January can be quite humorous (believe it or not) and wonderfully stimulating. Be aware, though, that the Capricorn humour is dry and sometimes a little cynical. But if that appeals to you, then good times are ahead.

SAGITTARIUS + AQUARIUS
Fire + Air = Hot Air

Air and fire work well together, as happens in this match of Sagittarius and Aquarius. You both love a busy life, perhaps one would even say hectic, and are always on the go in both your personal and professional lives. You both love meeting people, being the centre of the social action, and seek out anything to do with clubs, theatres, outings and outdoor sports. Together you will feel synergistically connected and enjoy a bustling social life with each other.

Just as there are similarities, so must there be differences, too. Aquarians tend to go through the most incredibly unexpected shifts and changes in their lives and, if you are involved in a relationship with them, you may find it difficult to understand how such radical changes can happen in the blink of an eye. Aquarius is a little more aloof than you, quirky by nature and progressive in all their attitudes. Fortunately this doesn't worry you because you are happy to let people have their own views. Perhaps the saying 'live and let live' applies very well to you, Sagittarius.

Aquarians can be quite rebellious by nature and resist being stifled in any shape or form. They are likely to take off at the drop of a hat, leaving you high and dry and even broken hearted. They take a certain amount of pleasure in bucking authority and want to live life on their own terms, irrespective of what people think. You like freedom, too, but the Aquarian brand of freedom is unique and could even rattle your Sagittarian sensibilities from time to time. Think back to the stage show *Hair*; hippies, free love and the song Age of Aquarius. These should put you in the picture.

With its electric energies, the planet Uranus, which rules Aquarius, brings a great deal of vibrant energy to the sexual side of this relationship combination. You are both exploratory when it comes to matters of intimacy, so there will be a constantly evolving relationship in the bedroom to your mutual satisfaction.

Aquarians born between the 21st and the 30th of January will surprise you by just how strong willed they can be. A clash of minds is likely with them, so you need to take extra precautions if you are serious about an association with this group. Mental flexibility will be required if you are to pursue a relationship with these Aquarians.

Aquarians born between the 31st of January and the 8th of February are affected by Gemini and Mercury, which happen to rule your marriage sector. You may hear the distant peal of wedding bells if you team up with an Aquarian from this group and they can bring you great fulfilment.

You may be drawn romantically to those Aquarians born between the 9th and the 19th of February, particularly if you're born between the 23rd of November and the 1st of December. The romantic and lucky Venus will help them to soothe your soul because it also co-rules their birth. In their company you'll feel loved, cherished and cared for.

SAGITTARIUS + PISCES
Fire + Water = Steam

Jupiter, your benevolent ruler, also rules Pisces and because of this the lucky vibrations of this planet extend to both of your lives. This is a particularly favourable omen and, with love, it brings good fortune. You have much in common and will be romantically attracted to each other, having similar ways of thinking.

Sagittarius and Pisces have a natural and intuitive link, combining spiritual and sensitive elements due to the vibrations of your ruling planet. You are both magnanimous in spirit, and share many of your feelings and thoughts with each other.

Pisces is also strongly influenced by Neptune, which makes them dreamy, sensitive and even mystical. Pisces, being the last of the zodiac signs, is incredibly psychic and sometimes considered the most evolved among us. They have a knack of knowing what you're thinking and planning and you can't hide your intentions from these individuals. This appeals to you, Sagittarius, because you also feel there's a deeper meaning to life. Philosophy, culture and higher thinking are the common ground between you.

As with most relationships you also have some differences that are worth noting. You, Sagittarius, have a fiery energy that may be a little too intense for the receptive and easygoing Pisces. You live life in the fast lane and this could make Pisces cringe at the speed with which you tackle anything and everything. Pisces is a dreamer, living in a world of spiritual ideas, and needs time for those dreams to manifest. You, on the other hand, would rather implement dreams than just dream them. These two diametrically opposed attitudes could erode the fabric of this relationship.

Pisces are nurturers and carers and you'll never be in need of anything should you choose to spend the rest of your life with them. You'll always be loved and supported by them in their own way. It would be a challenge indeed to get them to think practically or in the way that the average person does, but that is another matter altogether.

You are also similar in your sexual and emotional aspirations, so you can expect a very fulfilling physical interplay. Sexually speaking you are both extremely compatible and there can be some exciting moments, both inside and outside the bedroom!

You could have very similar interests to Pisces born between the 20th of February and the 28th or the 29th of February. These Pisceans have an intuitive streak, so listen closely when they get a hunch because it is usually correct.

Pisceans born between the 1st and the 10th of March will be finicky about the way you should save or spend money. Being as free and easy as you are, Sagittarius, this won't be an easy adjustment should you choose to make the attempt. They are emotional and their sensitivity may be a little too much for you to deal with.

A positive experience can be gained with those Pisceans born between the 11th and the 20th of March. Mars, Pluto and Jupiter influence their personalities. There are some secretive elements to this relationship, so be prepared for an unusual if not offbeat type of relationship if you're serious about an involvement with them.

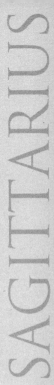

2011:
The Year Ahead

The only way of finding the limits of the possible is by going beyond them into the impossible.

— Arthur C. Clarke

Romance and friendship

It's very important not to get carried away with your relationships in 2011, Sagittarius. You'll be bubbly, confident and possibly a little over-enthusiastic about romance, particularly in the first part of the year.

There may be hidden factors associated with your love life, notably in January, with Venus and the Moon moving through your zone of secrets and hidden agendas. If you're not open to their existence at this point in time, you may miss very important signals that will set the trend for the rest of the year.

Certainly, being light-hearted and confident is a good thing, but not at the expense of being aware of how other people are feeling in the relationship.

By the 16th of January, when Mars moves to your zone of communication in your horoscope, you'll be better equipped to understand and listen to what your spouse or partner may have to say. You'll feel energetic about resolving your differences during this cycle and, up until the 20th of January, when the Sun also enters the picture, you can expect a great deal of communication, insight and resolution to any sort of conflicts that may be plaguing you.

The big transit for Sagittarius is the entry of Jupiter into your zone of love affairs on the 23rd of January. This heralds a one-year transit that expands and energises not just your personal, romantic or sexual relationships, but your creative skills as well. This is generally considered one of the better astrological aspects. So expect some good luck throughout 2011!

In February, your social life could bog you down a little due to the influence of Saturn in your zone of friendships. You may become more serious with respect to your friendships and will not want to entertain light-hearted or casual involvements. Perhaps you're seeking the deeper meaning of your friendships because of this transit.

This may be an important period in your life, to remove the dead wood from your social, personal or family lives. In this way you could consider using the classic tough love approach. If you're being used or abused and need to make a break, the testing influence of Saturn will most definitely make this difficult for you. But in the long run, if you're prepared to bite the bullet, you'll feel so much more empowered by your move away from these disruptive and disempowering people and influences.

Family affairs are strongly pronounced in February and March. This year, with Mars also entering the combination, you need to be careful not to let words exasperate you. You're likely to retaliate at the drop of a hat. Using cool, reflective responses is the better way to proceed, even if certain family members rub you up the wrong way.

A new and exciting romance may begin for you if you're not already involved after the 12th of March, when Uranus bears upon your romantic zone. Even if you are in a relationship, this planet revolutionises your approach to love and it means that you'll be ready, willing and able to try something completely different. This is a time of throwing away worn, outdated concepts and attempting something bold and adventurous in love.

You are impulsive and impatient during March, but fortunately, with the steadying influence of Saturn, you're not likely to do anything completely disadvantageous to yourself. However, I still issue a modest warning for you to tread lightly and not do things that are completely out of character. When the Sun enters your zone of love affairs on the 21st of March, you'll feel an upswing in creative energy and will want to connect with someone on an artistic or even possibly a philosophical platform.

April is a huge month for love and social activity for Sagittarians, as shown by the large number of planets congregating in that area of your horoscope. One thing you need to be mindful of is your inability to see facts clearly while making decisions during this phase, and this is due to the retrogressed movement of the planet Mercury. Don't give quick answers to questions you really need to think through more carefully. This might relate to meeting someone new, being swept off your feet, and not balancing your head with your heart.

With Mars, Uranus, the Sun, Jupiter and Mercury together in this zone of your horoscope, it's likely you may have more than one suitor looking to connect with you romantically. There may be some hard decisions that you have to make.

The health and wellbeing of a friend or lover may be of concern to you throughout the early part of May. If this is not directly a crisis in health, you could expect considerable discussion centring on you assisting them to become more aware of the importance of their diet, a healthy lifestyle and living in harmony with nature. Try not to force your opinion on them, however, because this is the classic case of retaliation based upon another person's ego.

Your perception of the world is dramatically changing and your interactions with others will also step up a notch towards the end of May, when the Sun enters your zone of marriage and public relations. It's a time to get out there, shine and show the world what you're made of.

Along with the Sun's transit through your marital sector in May, the important solar eclipse in June highlights what I've just spoken of with respect to dealing with others and your nearest and dearest. A solar eclipse is a very powerful celestial phenomenon that can shake things up dramatically. During this phase you'll need to look more carefully at your relationships and get real with yourself.

Your sexual affairs are strong throughout July and, with Mars opposing your Sun sign by the 13th, you may not only be desirous of sexual intimacy, but may demand it. Just remember, there's more than one way of doing things, and using tact and diplomacy may be the better option during this Mars transit.

Don't expect others to understand you that easily in August. You have to speak clearly and repeat yourself a couple of times, even if you think at first that what you said is plain enough. The action of Neptune, especially on family members and relatives, can be rather nebulous and misunderstandings are likely to occur. This may more likely be the case if your expectation of others is not being met by their behaviour or their responses. Be more realistic and understand that, especially with aged people in your family, a leopard rarely changes its spots.

Although others may see you as being a little more serious throughout September, there's a certain dignity being emanated by you. This will give others a sense of security and stability in your company. There is a calming influence by Saturn on your Sun sign at this time, which is just as well because Mars simultaneously enters your ninth zone of adventure, higher learning and travels.

In October and November Mars continues its ascent through your horoscope, signifying its dominance over your personality and your activities generally. You have a drive to be number one and, although this is normally connected with your career, it will have a strong bearing on your personal life as well. Most noticeable is the square or right-angle aspect to Jupiter, which tells us of your excessive or perhaps even wasteful lifestyle in these last few months of the year.

Pull yourself together; continue to use the steadying influence of Saturn as a counterbalance to these exaggerated energies of Mars and Jupiter. I say this because Jupiter's presence in your zone of health can indicate that these lifestyle imbalances may end up affecting your general physical and emotional wellbeing.

The progression of Venus and Saturn tells us that you may be feeling somewhat trapped in a relationship and, as November comes around, you may want to try something completely out of the ordinary. As long as this doesn't encroach on your moral or ethical standards, you should attempt to try something different and explore the possibilities in your relationship.

If you're in a committed marriage or de facto relationship and your partner is willing to work on the principles of the discovery of love and intimacy, then in general this will be a very productive period in your relationship and should cement the bonds of love deeply and for the long-term. In other cases, where there is a disparity between you and the other, it may be time to move on and explore life on your own.

Mars once again dominates the landscape of Sagittarians in December, the last month of 2011.

Mars is one of the better planets for Sagittarian-born natives, and highlights the fact that your independence, your drive and your popularity will be strong right up until the end of the year.

Work and money

Although you may be driven to work extremely hard in the first part of 2011, the frustrating thing may be the position of Saturn in your zone of profits, indicating a slower and steadier stream of income than what you'd prefer.

We see in January that Pluto, the Sun, Mars and the Karmic Point, the North Node, are all associated with your second zone of money, finance and income. You have an immense drive to earn more than you normally do, but the right angle from Saturn obstructs you. My first piece of advice, particularly in the first part of the year, is to go with the flow and not allow these planets to create unnecessary frustration for you.

The speculative influences of Jupiter and Uranus in February are strong. You have courage and determination, and Mars and Saturn enter into a more favourable aspect at this time, giving you the confidence to move forward and try something different, even a little bold.

Don't let the positions of Neptune, Mars, the Sun, Mercury, Uranus and Jupiter in the lower part of your horoscope deter you from working hard to achieve your goals. These planets in the lower portion of your horoscope simply mean you will be withdrawing of some of your outward-bound energies, regrouping, collecting and then focusing your attention on where you really want to go. In this manner you won't scatter your energies. Around May and June you can make some real headway in your work environment and improve your people skills as well.

A new level of understanding can be reached by June and July, and this will relate primarily to the way you interact with people and the world in general. You have the ability to understand intuitively what others want and can capitalise on it through your business deals and negotiations.

August and September are wonderful months for acquiring a better position in your work, communicating your ideas and gaining respect due to the transit of Mercury and Venus in the upper part of your horoscope. Venus and the Sun highlight some of your 'glory' in September, when they transit your tenth zone of success, career and ambition. You mustn't delay asking for a promotion—or indeed a pay rise—at this time, if that's what's on your mind.

In this last phase of the year, a grand trine between the Sun, Pluto and Jupiter and the earth signs is a notable configuration, denoting plenty of opportunity in your workplace. Just be careful that you don't push too hard because your ambitions may become insatiable. Use the element of earth to ground yourself and to achieve your objectives with a practical foundation. In this manner, you'll gain the support of both your co-workers and your superiors alike.

Jupiter's influence on your sixth zone of work may also point to the fact that you could be overdoing things. If you're working hard, you may be working a little too hard; you must remember to balance your work with some leisure time as well.

With Mars transiting your zone of education, higher learning and travels in October and in the early part of November, you might want to rethink the idea of educating yourself and learning some new skills to further your professional life. This may not necessarily be confined to courses and educational institutions as such, but could be expanded to include connecting with mentors, experts in the field you happen to work, and others who have a breadth of knowledge that you can draw upon to improve your own position in life.

In November the Sun, Mercury and Venus move to the low-key twelfth zone of your horoscope. It's best to do your work in private and not share too much of your trade secrets or your intellectual property with others, even those whom you consider trustworthy and close.

There's a principle at work here that has to do with containing your energy, collecting that power and directing it so that you can have maximum impact when you're ready to move forward. That seems to be what these three planets are highlighting in your life at this time.

In the latter part of November and December, you need to use the energies of Mars wisely, not dominating your co-workers or employees if you happen to be in a position of authority. By using your power wisely you can achieve great things and tie up many loose ends.

You'll be decisive, energetic and respected as a leader in your field. This is an excellent way to conclude 2011 and is a promise of even better things for you in 2012, Sagittarius.

Karma, luck and meditation

The prominent planets for you this year are Saturn, Mars and Jupiter. Saturn's influence on your zone of life-fulfilling events and income are slow and steady, but sure. Saturn gains considerable dignity by transiting its exalted sign of Libra throughout all of 2011. This indicates good fortune through older friends, people with wisdom and those who also have some spiritual insights as well. Try to think outside the square when socially connecting with those who are older, because this is a key to your success and good karma in 2011.

Mars has considerable power throughout 2011; but in particular, its strength in March, April, July, November and December is notable and will bring you the opportunities you seek. With self-initiative, much of your luck during these periods will be brought about by your own actions, especially in the last two months of the year, when Mars moves into the upper portion of your horoscope. You can expect some good fortune in your work, your education and your finances as well.

Jupiter brings with it some extraordinary opportunities when it passes into the fifth zone of love affairs at the end of January and early in February. Its proximity to the sudden and unexpected Uranus means that some of your relationships will undergo some transformations that even you hadn't expected.

By the same token, this also means chance meetings will occur that will stimulate and excite you as well. Someone you meet at this time may be a lucky rabbit's foot for you. Don't let your past habits judge others who seem a little bit out of the ordinary. Be open enough and prepared to explore the many different characters who could come your way and bring you good fortune in 2011.

Your spiritual and karmic enrichment is shown predominately by the Sun and Pluto, as well as, to a large extent, Mars. There are excellent opportunities in August and September to further your spiritual endeavours. This is the transit of the Sun and Venus in your ninth zone of spirituality and tenth house of personal achievement. Work hard on your meditative practices and connect with your higher self.

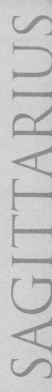

SAGITTARIUS

Your Bonus 2010 Three Month Forecast

OCTOBER
2010

Highlights of the month

From the 1st to the 4th, your responsibilities weigh heavily upon you and you mustn't make any commitment you can't keep. You must first be honest with yourself before you can be honest with others, so if you know in your heart of hearts that you can't deliver, don't say 'yes'.

Your mind is completely scattered between the 5th and the 7th and this is due to the combined influence of Uranus and Mercury. These two planets activate your restlessness and make it hard for you to concentrate or achieve any lasting results in your work.

Speak with friends between the 8th and 11th because they can open new doors and help you connect with an alternative network of people. This has equal value socially as much as commercially. This is a time when you can mix a little business with pleasure.

At the same time a brother or sister may need some assistance, so try to give them at least a little bit of your time during their period of need. You could also reconnect with someone from your past—an acquaintance, an old school friend or just someone from your old peer group—who just happens to reappear out of nowhere.

Between the 12th and the 14th, a lover or close friend exits stage left and may disappear for a while or at least be scarce and stop calling. Be patient and allow them the space they need to go through what they're going through.

You may be forced to make a journey or travel for some unpleasant reason between the 16th and the 19th. This may be a family issue and it's quite likely unavoidable. Do the best with the resources and abilities that are at your disposal.

You can be very dynamic and want the world to know it between the 22nd and the 25th. A desire to try something new or challenging will be scratching away at you. You will grow mentally during this period but may feel a bit impatient with others who are not quite as motivated or mentally exciting.

A letter or phone call will stimulate you between the 26th and the 30th. Your passion is to experience more but you may not be completely clear on what you want. You mustn't play mind games with others but rather should sidestep anyone whom you know isn't being straightforward with you.

Romance and friendship

You'll have to deal with some news relating to a relative who may be having problems in their relationships between the 5th and 7th. It could be news of a separation or divorce, the cause of which reminds you of your own situation. This event could give you some food for thought and a wake-up call if you've become lazy in dealing with similar matters in your own life.

Your personality and that of a friend may be at odds between the 8th and 11th. Simply accept the fact that there are differences between you and each can't force the other to be a clone. Don't lose it over conflicting opinions.

A friend who is thoroughly sick and tired of giving their all to someone they love may lean on you for some advice between the 12th and 18th. However, your advice seems to be falling on deaf ears and you could find yourself reaching a point of severe frustration. You must realise that sometimes people have to experience their own difficulties to learn their karmic lessons.

Around the 23rd your most significant other, such as a spouse or long-term lover, may reveal something to you about what's going on in their world. If there are blind spots in your relationship and you haven't been altogether aware of what happens in their work or personal social life, this will be an eye-opener for you. Remember that reinventing your relationships takes a lot of time and effort.

Be prepared to pay additional attention to your loved ones and friends between the 25th and 31st. You realise that things are meant to improve but only if you put in the prerequisite energy. You'll be spending considerable time looking at new perspectives and ways of propelling your love life forward. This is the time to get out and about in a bookshop and pick up some of those self-help, pop psychology or relationship rescue books that are on the shelves. You'll be ready for and receptive to what's on offer.

Work and money

You can gain through another person's loss around the 4th. By this I mean that if you are in the right position professionally when someone exits quickly, it could be time for you to step into their shoes. Don't forget, however, that this may be a tall order and you need to be reasonably confident you are up to the task and able to fulfil the role as adequately as the person who will no longer be there.

Your key words between the 7th and 10th are frugality, seriousness and concentrated work practices. Things are likely to occur slowly and you mustn't push for fast results. The prevailing trends demand that you act more slowly and deliberately to get the best possible results.

Between the 12th and the 15th you'll be focused on setting aside money for a rainy day so you'll be able to weather the storm of uncertain financial times. You can be progressive without being speculative. Study up on new ways to make money and to save as well.

Between the 23rd and 28th, you need to draw a line in the sand and set parameters as to what time you are going to allocate to work, and what time you'll allocate to recreation, rest and quality moments with the ones you love. This will be a period where you are trying to create greater harmony between these important facets of your life.

Destiny dates

Positive: 22, 29, 30, 31

Negative: 1, 2, 11

Mixed: 4, 5, 6, 7, 8, 9, 10, 12, 13, 14, 15, 16, 17, 18, 23, 24, 25, 26, 27, 28

Highlights of the month

You have some difficult choices in November when Venus, which has a strong bearing on your friendships, moves into a compromising position whereby you may need to refuse the requests of someone to help them financially. There may be other forms of compromise as well, for example, you may be requested to keep a secret that might go against your moral fibre.

You must trust your intuition in that moment and not rely on book knowledge or past religious standards to come to your conclusion. If you are unable to meet the needs of this friend, Saturn certainly indicates that you may have to part ways permanently. This could be the issue that was raised earlier in the year and now comes back for its final resolution.

There's nothing worse than feeling obscure or unnoticed. Between the 1st and the 4th, you may feel a little under the weather in this respect.

However, you mustn't for a minute assume that if you're not invited to some function, it's because you've done something wrong. The reasons may not be clear immediately, but don't beat yourself up over it. This cycle will pass fairly quickly and things will get back to normal.

You may not have too much of an inclination to work during this same period. Spending time with yourself seems more attractive than being with others. Spiritual strength can be gained just now, so take it as a lesson to improve the inner part of your character.

You're lucky in your communications between the 5th and the 9th and should get some sort of good break. This is a favourable time for meetings, interviews or other important get-togethers. Rather than speaking too much, let your magnetic personality do the talking for you.

The 10th to the 14th brings to you several romantic opportunities. Even if you're married, the two of you can restate your love for each other. Why not do that by taking off to a romantic getaway, which will be great for your relationship?

During the period of the 18th to the 25th, Mars dominates you but also endangers you at the same time. Watch your step. Drive carefully and don't argue over trifles with others. No good will come of it. It's best to avoid arguments, even though you have the upper hand. It takes more control to hold back than to let fly!

Jealousy should be completely rooted out between the 26th and the 30th. Even if you think that what you're saying isn't exactly possessive, others will take it that way. On the contrary, be generous and give others their freedom. They will come back to you eventually, and this way you'll know that being with you hasn't been forced upon them.

Romance and friendship

You will finetune your correspondence skills between the 1st and 4th, which will involve discussing some abstract or philosophical ideas. This is a great mental exercise but can also further cement your friendships with people near and far.

On the 6th and 7th self-control is absolutely necessary and working with older people means you can learn about others and yourself. At first you may feel inferior about how much they know, but don't forget you are younger, and that is par for the course.

On the 8th, spontaneous actions will certainly allow you to let off considerable emotional steam, but you may irritate others in the process. Keep a lid on it.

Between the 9th and 13th you could be nervous about meeting someone; maybe a romantic possibility? You can try to give your emotions free rein, but unfortunately you might also still feel uncomfortable until you get to know the person better.

On the 14th and 15th pleasant moods characterise these days, and contacts with women in particular will give you a feeling of connectedness.

On the 19th both Jupiter and Venus move in their direct motion, which is an astrological go-ahead for you to implement your ideas, irrespective of what others think or feel about them. This is a period of moral certitude and makes you feel comfortable with the decisions you make.

Between the 21st and 23rd you should quickly resolve any outstanding issues. If you procrastinate you will miss the boat and, because you are so restless, it is important for you to move into the new year with a clean slate, having cleared any emotional baggage out of the picture. You will be quite impatient to get your message across, that's for sure.

From the 25th to 29th, go out and purchase jewellery, clothing and other fashion accessories that will make you shine in the crowd. You want to be noticed and loved, but by the same token, remember you also have the chance to pick up a bargain or two after the Christmas rush is over.

Work and money

Between the 2nd and 8th you mustn't let others dictate how to do your work. You should stand firm on your ideas and principles knowing full well you have the experience and the desire to do your work in a way that befits you.

From the 10th to the 15th it's a good idea to relax in your role. Overcoming tensions means more productivity and this will be a period when you can achieve a lot.

A co-worker may become much friendlier than you expect between the 17th and 22nd. Do they have some ulterior motive? Probably not, but it's best to remain cautious.

Between the 26th and 30th there could be a conflict of interests in your business affairs. You may sense some hidden agenda, so tread warily.

Destiny dates

Positive: 14, 15, 17

Negative: 24

Mixed: 1, 2, 3, 4, 5, 6, 7, 8, 9, 10, 11, 12, 13, 18, 19, 20, 21, 22, 23, 25, 26, 27, 28, 29, 30

Highlights of the month

Between the 1st and the 5th, money concerns will overwhelm you. You may not have the time to manage them all, so why not get some help? You need to delegate some of the financial tasks, especially if you're trying to make heads or tails of a taxation requirement.

From the 6th to the 8th your energy is again high and physical exercise is not a bad idea. Why not sign up for a new gym membership? Are you aware that some health funds even allow you to make a claim against this type of expense? Look into that. You can kill two birds with one stone, those being financial savings and improved health.

You must check and recheck your statements between the 10th and the 14th. There may be errors you've overlooked, but these can actually work in your favour. You'll find yourself with a healthier bank balance once you identify where those errors are.

The period leading up to Christmas, particularly between the 15th and the 19th, may be full of tension. Try to decompress the family situation rather than inflaming it with your opinions. Why not act as a peacemaker rather than a troublemaker during this festive season?

Lunar and solar eclipses are some of the most important astrological developments this month. With the powerful lunar eclipse occurring on the 21st, it will grill you to sort out any lingering marital or romantic problems. Certain revelations may be hard to stomach, but once these surface and are removed from the picture, your relationship will be so much better.

Mercury excites you between the 22nd and the 30th. Your love of travel and adventure means that you'll have to get away, feeling it's necessary to finish the year with an escape to a beautiful and peaceful location. What a wonderful way to conclude 2010!

Romance and friendship

Between the 2nd and 6th a sense of duty to your family causes you to sidestep social offers. In any case, you'll prefer your own company so it's not a bad idea to just lay low for a while until your energy is back on track.

Between the 7th and 10th, learning about your family history, your genealogy, is an advantage because it will help you to understand yourself. You'll find photographs, notebooks and other family paraphernalia fascinating.

Neighbours in this period may act strangely, but it's best for you to bite your tongue for the sake of peace.

From the 14th to the 20th it's not a bad idea to make a show of your strength without pouncing. Flexing your muscles to avoid a future problem is a wise move. Children will need directing, and vehicles and other entertainment items may need to be fairly shared, which can also present its own set of problems inasmuch as who gets what and when.

Between the 24th and 30th Christmas will be enjoyable with numerous friends and lots of fun. Older members of the community cross your path and befriending them will make you feel less stressful for some strange reason. Enjoy the closing part of 2010 fully!

Work and money

Between the 5th and 10th finish off negotiations and don't create any more work for yourself. Prepare for some well-deserved time off.

Mercury and Pluto indicate that you may want to make money or prestige a reason for an argument with someone between the 14th and 20th. That's not a particularly good idea. Show what you can do, not what you have. Trying to impress others with your wealth will not work and may in fact go against your best interests.

The eclipse of the 21st occurs in your partnership sector and indicates that you want a more diverse arrangement in your work, particularly with colleagues. Make it happen!

Between the 28th and 30th, expect extra profits to flow in. This providence will be a nice bonus to finish 2010!

Destiny dates

Positive: 22, 23, 24, 25, 26, 27, 28, 29, 30

Negative: 1

Mixed: 2, 3, 4, 5, 6, 10, 11, 12, 13, 14, 15, 16, 17, 18, 19, 20, 21

2011:
Month By Month
Predictions

JANUARY 2011

If you would create something, you must be something.

— Johann Wolfgang von Goethe

Highlights of the month

During January, Jupiter and Uranus provide you with ample opportunities, if not lucky circumstances, especially in your domestic sphere. They are indicators that you may be on the verge of changing your living circumstances and may come across something that is a perfect fit for you at this stage of your life.

For those of you who don't necessarily want to move, you can beautify your home and really start creating a space that makes you feel comfortable, peaceful and capable of creating the life that you want for yourself and for those whom you love. Apart from this, you may be the recipient of some sort of gift or opportunity that you hadn't been expecting.

With the Sun in a hard aspect to Saturn after the 15th, things could get a little heavy, especially regarding your responsibilities and obligations. Rest assured that the Sun's movement is rapid, so this shouldn't last too long. It could centre on your friendships and may be related to some outstanding debt to a friend that you don't necessarily want to repay just yet. However, the sooner you do, the better for everyone concerned.

The full Moon on the 19th occurs in your zone of sexuality and personal transformation, which will spill over into your relationships. This highlights the fact that you are working hard, along with your partner or spouse (if you happen to be married), to create a more loving relationship and one in which intimacy becomes the cornerstone.

At the same time, Mercury and Pluto also underpin this full Moon by leading you to investigate more seriously the things within your communication style that could be obstructing a happier and fulfilling relationship.

By the 20th, the excellent aspect between the Sun and Jupiter brings with it a wealth of feeling and positive emotions that are shared between you and your loved ones, bringing healing and greater opportunities for growth in your partnerships.

It's an exciting time for you after the 23rd, when Jupiter enters your zone of love affairs. Mind you, this is an important transit because of Jupiter's slow-moving orbit, which takes approximately twelve years to return back to this position. You should note this and take full advantage of the opportunities that present themselves to you.

During this same time frame, Venus and Saturn stabilise your relationships and this is a time when, even if you don't feel completely 'excited' about your love life, you'll feel more secure and loving in a more practical way.

In the last few days of the month, try to think clearly before opening your mouth. You're likely to need a little bit of extra time to come to a decision or a conclusion before making a commitment.

Romance and friendship

If you have begun a relationship that is somewhat new, from the 1st until the 3rd of January, you must keep your eyes and ears open to discover how the person deals with responsibilities. This is a testing period and you'll want to study each other's attitudes to life generally.

Between the 4th and the 6th, one of you may feel more passionate than the other, or particularly interested in self-satisfaction rather than relating to each other sympathetically.

Friendships bog you down around the 8th, when the Sun and Saturn create difficult aspects to each other. Someone with whom you are normally close doesn't pull their weight around this time and that could bother you, making you feel quite withdrawn and angry. Try not to let it upset you too much.

Going for a long trip is necessary from the 9th till the 12th, because you could be feeling smothered by your normal group of friends or family members.

Also, communications with those who live at a distance is also on the cards because Mercury fully activates your speech and intellectual capacities.

The finger of fate is pointing at you between the 14th and the 17th and you may finally have to deal with someone or something that you've ignored for a considerable period of time. It's better to do what you have to do and not avoid this issue any longer.

Romance is excellent for you from the 23rd till the 26th, with Jupiter entering your zone of love affairs. A steadying effect from Venus and Saturn also ensures that romance and social activities run smoothly.

The 27th till the 31st is also a great time to share your feelings with friends, but be more deliberate in what you have to say because there could be the odd misunderstanding between you.

Work and money

You're likely to receive what you asked for between the 1st and the 5th of January, but it's important for you to have a clear definition of what you want the end result to be. Otherwise, those whom you approach may be confused as to what it is you're after, precisely. By giving shape to your goals and objectives early in the year, you're more likely to achieve your ambitions.

You're able to persuade others in your working life from the 7th until the 11th. As well as having strong communication skills, the added charm of

Venus makes you lovable and people won't be able to say 'no' to the offers you place on the table. Try not to rely too much on your good looks or your attire, however, because you need to prove you are a capable worker as well.

Between the 20th and the 24th, why not create some of your own rules if you feel as though you're being cornered by 'the system' or conservatives around you? This will precipitate some unusual happenings that bring with them some additional, unexpected successes.

With a few hiccups in contractual arrangements around the 26th, you can finalise your dealings between the 27th and the 31st by reaching a win–win situation for all concerned.

Destiny dates

Positive: 4, 5, 6, 7, 19, 20, 21, 22, 23, 24, 25, 27, 28, 29, 30, 31

Negative: 14, 15, 16, 17

Mixed: 1, 2, 3, 8, 9, 10, 11, 12, 26

Highlights of the month

Such things as communication, siblings, close neighbours and your general day-to-day movements to and from work may be spotlighted quite strongly in the month of February, especially after the 2nd. You may wish to change the way you talk to others, to gain a greater understanding of your own and others' thinking processes for the purpose of improving your relationships. Some astrologers agree that this is also a very powerful educational aspect because it influences your thinking mind.

During the first week of the month you will also feel somewhat excited about your relationships but you need to be careful that you don't do something that is out of character.

You want to exercise your Sagittarian freedom just now. With these planets, especially with Mercury influencing you as well around the 3rd, you'll want to prove that you are different, capable of thinking laterally and able to do things for no other reason than for their shock value. Try to remember the context of your speech and where you are before saying something that could cause you to get egg on your face.

From the 4th until the 7th, you'll be focused very much on finances again and will find ample opportunities to somehow increase your income at this stage. There are some excellent planetary influences happening at the moment: especially on the 5th, when contracts can favour you; on the 6th when publishing and self-promotion will work wonders for you; and once again on the 7th, when Mars and Saturn provide you constructive outlets for your creative enterprise.

Don't be disappointed after the 15th if some of your travel plans don't come off. You may have other, more pressing commitments that preclude you from making the break at the time you had anticipated. The Sun and Neptune around the 17th also point to this fact, and could show that you're rather confused about the destination, the costs, or other issues such as some of the people with whom you may wish to travel.

You feel cold, alone and disconnected from friends, but more importantly from lovers, around the 19th and the 21st. It could be that you need a little space for yourself rather than trying too hard to receive the approval and the love you desire from others. Look within yourself to find your own satisfaction.

After a brief lull in your energies between the 19th and the 21st, Mercury and Mars kick-start you around the 22nd into some feverish activity. However, your speech and mind could be so quick that you leave others behind. Be more sensitive to the pace at which others think and work.

Mars enters your zone of domestic circumstances after the 23rd and cautions you to be less impulsive in dealing with members of your family.

Romance and friendship

If there are disagreements at home on the 2nd and the 3rd of February, it could be your important job to decompress the situation and act as a mediator between relatives who are at war.

Exciting friendships are part of your destiny between the 4th and the 5th. You may meet someone who inspires you and find yourself talking at considerable length about topics in which you probably didn't even think you had an interest.

The period of the 6th till the 10th is perfect for advertising yourself to dating sites and other online services if you are looking to make contact with someone new. You may also be invited to partake in an event (or a blind date) that could prove satisfying.

Mars and Saturn make friendships constructive between the 12th and the 13th, but by the 14th you could find yourself being a little too obsessive about some facet of someone's behaviour. This could cause you to become involved in a disagreement. Try to be the peacemaker and not the warrior.

From the 15th till the 19th your intuition is quite strong and you can sense what others are feeling and thinking. Use this to your advantage but don't push too hard around the 19th, when Venus and Saturn could cause you to step on someone's toes emotionally.

Home affairs are happy and fulfilling between the 20th and the 21st. It's a good time to plan a family reunion and enjoy the company of relatives whom you may not have seen for some time.

From the 22nd up until the 26th you may find yourself in a fluster if an unannounced visitor lands on your doorstep and you haven't yet cleaned the house or made it presentable enough.

Differences in philosophical views could get in the road of friendships between the 27th and the 28th. Respect others for their opinions.

Work and money

You may be confused about your role between the 1st and the 3rd of February, but when the new Moon occurs in your zone of communications on the 4th, it's all systems go in your work. Push hard for contracts and agreements and don't take 'no' for an answer.

The 5th till the 8th is a constructive time, but don't burn yourself out around the 7th. You may be burning the candle at both ends and need to work much more closely with mentors or employers to figure out an agenda that doesn't tire you out too much.

Mercury and Saturn provide you with a slow but steady stream of income and if, around the 14th, you're careful enough and you don't sweep too much of your spendthrift nature under the carpet, you can start to see some positive benefits for your savings plan.

Legal matters will only escalate if you don't pay attention to details between the 17th and the 19th. Do what needs to be done to avoid arguments.

Real estate matters are strongly favoured around the 20th, with foreign investments around the 22nd also taking up much of your attention.

If between the 23rd and the 28th you need to have some construction or service work done around your home, make sure you get good references rather than simply looking through the phone book. You could find yourself having to clean up a mess when someone's skills don't quite end up matching what they said they were.

Destiny dates

Positive: 4, 5, 6, 8, 9, 10, 12, 13, 16

Negative: None

Mixed: 1, 2, 3, 7, 14, 15, 17, 18, 19, 20, 21, 22, 23, 24, 25, 26, 27, 28

Highlights of the month

Contracts continue to seem attractive, due to the presence of Venus in your zone of communications and agreements. Notwithstanding the sweet and seductive tone of this planet, you must be on your guard. Mercury and the Sun give you a high degree of clear insight into the motivation of others and there's some hint of the Sun in your zone of secrets and hidden enemies, so there could be some ulterior motive to what others are saying or trying to do with you. Keep your wits about you.

Between the 4th and the 10th you have the drive, the get up and go and the physical prowess to enjoy some outdoor sports, physical exercise and the increased stamina in every aspect of your life. Mercury also gives you an additional creative fuel to enjoy life on many different fronts.

You are lucky from the 11th, when Venus and Jupiter, the two lucky benefits of the zodiac, bless you with respect to children, creative pursuits and possibly even some new love affair that could turn up with a soulmate. Don't turn a blind eye to the offers that come your way during these fortunate transits.

You may be looking in the wrong direction for answers after the 14th. You may have been led up the garden path by someone only to find that you have to retrace your steps and look in a completely different area for solutions. Anger, frustration and pointing the finger at someone else for your own errors could land you in even further trouble around the 15th.

After the 21st expect sudden meetings that bedazzle you. But these striking, chance meetings can also sometimes end just as quickly as they start. Don't expect too much from strangers you meet.

A love of knowledge, spiritual and cultural activities may dominate your mind and your activities after the 24th. The ninth zone of your horoscope reflects this and Venus, the planet of love, offers you an opportunity to explore these higher dimensions of human nature if you wish.

You're idealistic up until the 27th, showing your unconditional approach to love and communication. At this time you may wish to help someone who's in the doldrums and will gain some great satisfaction to rendering some selfless service to them.

On the 31st be mindful of the fact that Mercury, which enters into its retrograde movement, could present you with some rather ticklish problems and you are ill-advised to make a firm decision on any offer, purchase or other negotiation. Wait until you feel more settled mentally.

Romance and friendship

Between the 1st and the 4th of March you're more likely to want to stay home rather than go out on the town with friends. You'll find it easier to remain behind closed doors, thinking, reminiscing and being a little more sentimental than usual. The new Moon highlights important changes in your home life and the way you relate to relatives.

You could be worried between the 6th and the 11th and this has to do with your self-esteem. You need to work on yourself rather than asking others to bolster your ego. Anything that comes from outside yourself is rather shaky, so work on yourself, meditate, and build your character from within.

Watch yourself mentally, physically and emotionally between the 14th and the 16th. You'll be very impulsive but may also be in a rush to meet others or get to your destination on time. Remember that haste makes waste.

You're indecisive around the 19th. Don't let someone steer you off the course of your own standards or morality, or you may later regret the decision.

After the 21st your social life bubbles over, with loads of creative and romantic opportunities coming your way. For committed Sagittarians, this is a time when you can recreate your relationship.

You're a little out of step with some of your friends between the 24th and the 27th. You need to modernise your wardrobe, your hairstyle and even some of the ways you go about interacting socially. This will be hard but sometimes a revolution in your life is necessary to move forward.

You want to purchase some furniture or other objects of art that reflect your personality. This is a great idea, as long as you're not doing this simply as an ego boost. From the 28th to the 31st, continue to work on your personal strengths rather than on outward gestures.

Work and money

Seize opportunities quickly between the 2nd and the 4th of March. Venus and Uranus provide you with insights into new methods of doing things and possibly even new jobs that are available.

If you're a savvy investor, the 7th till the 12th is a wonderful time to put money into stocks, commodities and other long-term futures and investment strategies. If you're not clear on these matters, hire an investment broker or financial planner to help you.

The month peaks professionally and financially for you with the full Moon occurring in your zone of career on the 19th. You are emotionally tuned in to what you should be doing and feel a strong sense of purpose and destiny at this time.

It's best to wait until after the 21st to have important discussions with your employer or those who are hiring and firing.

You may have to postpone an important engagement around the 27th, but that doesn't necessarily mean that you've lost an opportunity. Reschedule it by the 30th, however, before Mercury goes retrograde.

Destiny dates

Positive: 1, 2, 3, 4, 5, 21, 28, 29, 30

Negative: 14, 15, 16

Mixed: 6, 7, 8, 9, 10, 11, 12, 19, 24, 25, 26, 27, 31

Highlights of the month

Your true Sagittarian spirit comes to the fore throughout April and this is evidenced by several planets in your zone of speculation. It's a well-known fact that a Sagittarian is one person who is keen on taking a punt in life, which is exactly what may happen throughout this month.

Jupiter is now favourably influencing your Sun sign and you must take full advantage of these powerful and beautiful energies that are making you popular, lucky and, I might add, also a little 'weightier'. Be careful what you eat because too much of a good thing can be detrimental and cause you to gain some weight.

There could be some confusing affairs mounting in your domestic space after the 4th. Older family members could be problematic or you may find it difficult to find a solution to some relationship problem that has plagued you for a while.

The solution to this could be the aspect of the Sun to your Sun sign and to Jupiter between the 5th and the 7th. Boldly declare your position and don't be afraid of hurting other people's feelings, especially if what you are offering them is the truth. By doing this you may upset them in the first instance, but at least everyone will know where you stand and this, to a large extent, will clear the clouds of confusion.

You'll have to deal with some unsavoury social circumstances after the 9th. Try not to let this get you down. You could feel like a fish out of water, being invited to something that is not necessarily your cup of tea but is nevertheless a social obligation that you must meet.

You can't sweep your emotional or social frustrations under the rug forever. The Mars–Saturn aspect is a challenging one after the 19th and relates to some problem associated with a friend. This period up until the 21st can be problematic for you, particularly if you are bottling up many feelings of discontent and resentment. Why not speak about how you feel and let those concerned know your position?

Due to the above transits, a healthy expression of these devitalising energies is essential, because the Sun will enter your zone of health after the 20th. If you're not careful, you could find that work, bottled up emotions and other grudges may start to undermine your sense of wellbeing.

Here's your chance to off-load this emotional baggage, clear your mind and get back on track through a healthy and positive lifestyle. Mercury goes direct on the 23rd, indicating that any confusion over a transaction or financial matter can be rectified now and you can move forward with a sense of purpose and positive outcome.

Romance and friendship

The period of the 1st up until the 3rd of April could see you fostering a new relationship or friendship. In fact, this is one of the best periods of the year to develop a soulmateship with someone. Even if someone doesn't seem to be your cup of tea, investigate this person's character a little more thoroughly. You may be surprised at the outcome.

From the 5th until the 9th you will have ample opportunity to interact socially with friends and strangers alike. However, you could feel a little awkward around the 9th, when Venus, in its hard aspect to your Sun sign, highlights some of your inadequacies, perhaps socially or with respect to etiquette. Brush up your skills in these areas first.

You are trying to be more independent—that is, less dependent on your friends and relatives—between the 12th and the 18th. But when the full Moon of the 18th occurs in your zone of friendships, you may realise just how dependent upon and appreciative of friends you are. Reconnect with those people who've been a solid, long-term supporter of yours. Re-establish the bonds of friendship, and celebrate.

You could speak a little too soon on the 20th. Measure your words carefully before giving a commitment. You are impatient to get things moving, only to find that the rules of the game have changed and that someone in the equation has moved the goal posts.

Others will look up to you after the 22nd. Mars empowers you and gives you a sense of drive and leadership. Your peer group may look up to you to help steer them as a group in the right direction. Your words of advice will be practical but also very enlightening.

You need to off-load some past habits around the 27th and the 28th. Don't let outdated forms of behaviour stifle you in your search for romantic happiness.

Work and money

With Jupiter's lucky hand resting on your shoulder between the 2nd and the 7th of April, you can do no wrong in your professional life. Do your work confidently but don't let others set the agenda or the pace. If you need to complete your tasks in a slower and more methodical manner, don't be hurried. It's during these moments of haste that you can err. Avoid cutting corners.

A conflict of business interests occurs between the 21st and the 24th. Make sure everyone is on the same page before you assume something and set the wheels of a process in motion.

Mercury goes direct on the 25th and, up until the 27th, you have the green light to say 'yes' to some contract or agreement with full confidence.

Having a positive mental attitude is well and good between the 28th and the 30th, but remember you also need to have the correct information for a project you're working on before you can boldly declare success.

Destiny dates

Positive: 1, 2, 3, 5, 6, 7, 12, 13, 14, 15, 16, 17, 25, 26, 27

Negative: 9, 19, 20, 21, 24

Mixed: 4, 18, 22, 23, 28, 29, 30

MAY
2011

Highlights of the month

It's time to get real about your health and diet. The new Moon this month heralds a turning point in your self-awareness and what is required to lead you into a healthy and more productive lifestyle. You will be feeling far more sensitive to the foods that you eat and to the environment and the people with whom you are in contact. You will start to sense the impact that these different factors have on your life and also on the way you make your decisions.

Your work will take precedence over many other things, too, and it could well be that your health, your diet and the way in which you conduct yourself professionally are strongly tied in with each other.

Between the 1st and the 5th you'll find yourself expending a lot of energy in your workplace. Up until the 11th you may be holding off doing what needs to be done and distracting yourself with other things that are not really important.

One of the most fortuitous astrological meetings is the conjunction of Venus and Jupiter and, this month, after the 12th, this combination occurs in your zone of romance. And added to that is communicative Mercury, giving its own touch of spice to this configuration.

A thoroughly wonderful opportunity occurs in your love life right now. Romance should shine. Friends should support you and love is definitely in the air! Don't hide yourself away from social engagements that give you the perfect chance to meet Mr or Mrs Right.

Yet again, Venus continues to send vibrant and lucky energies to you in your career and educational pursuits. Students should feel particularly lucky and their exam results should be better than expected. The middle of the month is an excellent time to focus on those subjects that have been causing you some dilemma.

Jupiter, after the 15th, brings with it some keen, intuitive understanding of problems in your educational sphere, and your marks should give you great confidence for the future. Some of you may want to take up a new form of education, so correspondence courses or Internet study could be of interest.

Watch your health after the 17th because you may be seeking excessive pleasure as a means of counterbalancing the workload I mentioned earlier in the month. The Sun is at a right angle to your ninth zone of ethics, morals and spiritual leanings.

After the 21st, when the Sun enters your marital zone, you'll find yourself reinvigorated by your partner's activities and will want to support him or her in their endeavours. There could be an overlap between their work and your romantic association with them, so you'll probably find yourself working in close quarters with those whom you love most.

Romance and friendship

The 2nd till the 6th of May highlights health issues for many Sagittarians. You may wonder how this has anything to do with your emotional or social connections, but it does.

Continuing to withhold and regret something and feeling guilty about it may be part of the cause of these erosive interior elements. Speak about how you feel, even if it's uncomfortable, because this will help provide the right internal environment for your health, wellbeing and peace of mind.

Favourable communications between the 7th and the 12th indicate the development of social connections that also involve you in some creative pursuits as well. Dealing with children may help revive your childlike innocence during this phase. Don't be scared to have fun, irrespective of what others think and say.

Do some shopping between the 13th and the 15th. Even if you spend a little more than your budget allows you'll be able to make a gift, a gesture of good faith to someone else, and rekindle the flame of friendship.

The health of a relative after the 17th could cause some worry for you. You needn't postpone all your other plans at this time but do make the effort at least to connect and show you're still a part of their life.

Be careful of arguments between the 21st and the 23rd. Pacify your partner rather than inflaming the situation, especially if you are tempted to say things that rile them up. When the Sun enters your zone of marriage and public relations on the 21st, you're more likely to see eye to eye with them.

Transformative processes in your relationships are shown by the harmonious blending of the Venus and Pluto energies in your horoscope after the 23rd. You and your lover are more likely to be in tune, prepared to tear down the walls of separation and to discard those habits that are hindering the growth of your relationship. Spiritual practices are spotlighted during this time.

From the 24th to the 30th your passions abound. You are likely to want to express the physical side of your nature, so set aside ample time to connect intimately with the one you love.

Work and money

You know you have to tighten your belt but, between the 1st and the 5th of May, you may opt to do the exact opposite and spend money with abandon, knowing full well that later you'll suffer the consequences. If you do that, enjoy it thoroughly.

From the 8th to the 12th you could be dissatisfied with elements of your working environment. You may also need to exercise additional caution in the operation of equipment, machinery and other electrical or technological devices. Problems arise through the malfunctioning of equipment. Review your systems and procedure manuals. Get advice on software or hardware issues.

Letter-writing communications and other forms of technical correspondence are highlighted between the 13th and the 17th. Putting out fires may preclude you from finishing some of your work on time. Elicit the help of subordinates or others. The key word at this time is delegation.

An excellent round of aspects from Mercury and the Sun bode well for your financial and contractual circumstances between the 21st and the 24th. Don't procrastinate on closing a deal. You can afford to be a little more pushy than usual.

Read the fine print before jumping to conclusions between the 27th and the 30th. Things may not be as bad as you at first think.

Destiny dates

Positive: 7, 24, 25, 26

Negative: 6

Mixed: 1, 2, 3, 4, 5, 8, 9, 10, 11, 12, 13, 14, 15, 16, 17, 18, 21, 22, 23, 27, 28, 29, 30

Highlights of the month

Your desire to improve your relationships reaches a pinnacle this month, with the new Moons on both the 1st and the 15th powerfully influencing your most important relationships in life.

You need to start afresh, even if you're in an existing relationship and, between the 1st and the 3rd, along with the solar eclipse, you will find yourself clearing out the dead wood and having an emotional spring cleaning of sorts. It will be critical for you to get your partner or spouse onside because there's no point in remaining stuck in the past.

Communication is high on the agenda after the 4th, with Mercury also prodding your partners—both personal and business—to engage in discussions with you. The problem you'll have is that Mercury and Neptune in a hard relationship to each other don't often make it easy for the words to come out perfectly.

It's nice to know that when Mars and Venus occupy the same location celestially, passion will abound. Your desire to perfect your work is highlighted by this fact. You'll be spending additional hours in your workplace or, if you're a home-maker, will want to clean up those unsightly areas in the house that have been bothering you for some time.

You have a sense that your environment reflects strongly on who you are and the opinions that people may have of you. Housework—even tidying up your own personal corner or those places that usually aren't viewed by the outside world—will need to be finished so you can have peace of mind and create some additional space for yourself.

If for some reason you haven't been able to resolve other people's problems completely, it may be time to say, 'enough is enough.' You needn't be harsh or cold-hearted in your manner, but you need to draw a line in the sand and let people know that you too have stuff to work through and that they should respect your desire for personal space as well.

A sense of self-empowerment can take place when the full Moon occurs in your Sun sign on the 15th. Things should change dramatically for you after this time and you'll be feeling more comfortable about philosophical versus practical affairs. Things should flow and your inner and outer lives should be more balanced.

Don't let Mercury and Uranus disrupt you between the 19th and the 22nd, when nervous tension could get the better of you. Think clearly and don't rush your decisions.

Work on a ticklish problem with a friend after the 23rd, but try not to involve yourself in too much alcoholic-based recreation. You could have an adverse reaction to it.

Romance and friendship

Between the 1st and the 3rd of June you may place too much emphasis on your philosophical differences with someone else. What's the point of arguing over opinions that probably won't change in the short-term, anyhow? Live and let live.

The new Moon on the 1st will be particularly important for most Sagittarians. For some who have already been engaged in a deeply committed relationship, this could be the next stage when marriage or a live-in situation takes place. For those of you looking for friendship or a soulmate, the new Moon indicates the start of new things.

Mercury and Neptune create confusion between the 4th and the 6th. Be clear about what you want to do; alert others to your plans so they can't blame you for not having been told. You want to avoid misunderstandings.

An old friend from the past could come back into the picture between the 9th and the 14th. Perhaps some of your karma hasn't yet been resolved and this is the perfect time—one on one, mind you—to get together to see whether the friendship can be improved.

You are keen to understand the mechanisms of sexuality between the 17th and the 20th. The *Kama Sutra*, Tantra and other esoteric or psychological insights into intimacy and how to improve your sexual experiences are spotlighted during this phase.

After the 22nd you could be in for a head-on confrontation with someone whom you normally get on well. Once again this has everything to do with the fact that you're pushing yourself too hard and blaming others for your circumstances.

You are wild and wacky between the 26th and the 30th and want to step outside your normal routine and way of doing things. And why not? This is what life is about and what the Sagittarian temperament stands for: adventure and a little bold living!

Work and money

On the 2nd, under the solar eclipse, you need to stand in the other person's shoes to understand where they're coming from properly. This is critical to your business and financial affairs in June. Don't make any assumptions because you're likely to miss the point completely.

In your meetings, make sure you have a clear agenda from the 5th to the 8th. You may find yourself talking around in circles simply for not having had a clear plan of what you want to achieve. Write memos with your expectations and circulate that to the attendees.

You have excellent opportunities for securing business deals after the 10th. Your popularity will ensure you don't have to do too much hard selling to win over the hearts of customers and clients.

Your creative endeavours prosper from the 13th up until the 20th. Try not to think too much about what the outcome will be during this period; rather, let your intuition and the universal processes perfecting your own creativity provide you with solutions. The key word in this period is trust.

Accept an invitation to a work function on the 30th. It will be lucky for you.

Destiny dates

Positive: 9, 10, 11, 12, 13, 14, 15, 16, 17, 18, 26, 27, 28, 29, 30

Negative: 23

Mixed: 1, 2, 3, 4, 5, 6, 7, 8, 19, 20, 21, 22, 25

Highlights of the month

Not all journeys are physical. This month, with Mercury positing your zone of travel, it's likely that the mental planet will create a desire in you to travel across more intellectual and spiritual platforms. This is a month of self-discovery, where you can look at those parts of your personality that heretofore have been hidden or in need some sort of positive adjustment.

Between the 1st and the 6th, you might feel a little disappointed at the comments of a friend regarding your personality or some of your personal habits. But if you look more carefully, you'll start to see that there are some benefits to this type of criticism, especially if they are constructive and are in the spirit of helping you rather than tearing you apart.

Venus is on the warpath between the 8th and the 11th. It has aspects to Uranus, Pluto and Jupiter. A sudden turn in affairs could be caused by some problems over money or debts. It's always a bad idea to mix friendships with finances, or business with pleasure. Venus and Jupiter in friendly aspect can help resolve this problem.

Mars, as usual, is steamy and impulsive after the 13th and may adversely affect your Sun sign. You must slow your pace, think carefully about your plans and not do too much because otherwise you could rush about, trip up and possibly even injure yourself. Mars is a warring planet and shows that you need to let off steam. But this has to be done in an appropriate manner, otherwise problems can ensue.

On the heels of this Mars aspect we see the double difficulty of Venus and Mercury on the rise, hinting that your responsibilities to loved ones may be breached, more as a form of retaliation and revenge rather than anything else. Please don't let childish emotions get in the way of your clear-sightedness.

The 22nd till the 30th is a wonderful time to allow the free expression of your emotional and creative talents. You can be enterprising as well by using these creative impulses in your workplace, especially around the 30th, when Mercury enters your career zone. This should be a lucky period for commencing workplace activities.

Romance and friendship

On the 1st, 2nd, 5th and 6th of July you have the opportunity to book either your travel tickets or perhaps even enrol in some sort of educational program for self-improvement. You are mindful of what needs to be done to improve your chances in the so-called 'social market'.

On the 7th, Mars and Saturn constructively bring you opportunities for love and romance, but initially the people you meet may seem a little dry and way too practical for your liking. Give these early meetings a chance to ripen before passing too harsh a judgement.

The unexpected behaviour of friends or family members between the 9th and the 12th comes as a shock and could leave you high and dry. The important lesson in these transits is how well you can manage your reactions to their behaviour. Remain calm and don't be over-sensitive to what happens.

Around the 13th your feelings could be cold and lonely. Someone is not giving you the affection you feel you deserve. Find your own happiness for a couple days until this transit passes.

From the 14th until the 18th you are less inwardly inclined and will be able to take the bull by the horns, socially speaking. There's no harm in initiating a date yourself, even if you feel that etiquette traditionally dictates that males should be the ones to ask first. You will have a positive response from the other party.

Deal with the psychological 'stuff' of your relationship, especially around the 28th, when something could arise in conversation that makes you feel uncomfortable.

If you have some disagreements about personal taste or affection and attention on the 30th, it's nothing to worry about. The situation will end amicably with you kissing and making up.

Work and money

Reorganisation will be one of your key words this month and, when Venus transits your eighth zone of transformations around the 4th of July, you should put your mind and heart into the job of cleaning out those cupboards, throwing out the old files and generally reducing the junk pile.

From the 6th and the 9th you must be careful not to divulge a secret or some piece of information that could damage the reputation of someone with whom you work. No matter how tempting, don't pass on that information! The buck will have to stop with you.

If you're feeling that business is a little slow between the 10th and the 18th, get out your old address book, call long-term clients and resuscitate some of your mainstream business dealings. You will be able to create some additional cash flow for yourself.

You can be more productive between the 28th and the 30th by taking on an exercise plan, especially if your company is offering one as a benefit of your employment policy. It will clear out your head, give you more energy and regenerate some of the passion for your work that may have been lost in the recent past.

Destiny dates

Positive: 22, 23, 24, 25, 26, 27, 29, 30

Negative: None

Mixed: 1, 2, 3, 4, 5, 6, 7, 8, 9, 10, 11, 12, 13, 14, 15, 16, 17, 18, 28

Highlights of the month

Much of your attention this month, particularly between the 5th and the 13th, could centre on changes to your career plans or modifications in the way you interact with work colleagues. There are some wonderful developments in your work-place that may have to do with some of the new contacts you make; people who offer you strategic changes.

Sometime after the 16th you may experience an upswing in your profitability and this could be by way of a gift, inheritance or some lucky win, perhaps through a lottery. You're also in a better position to negotiate a joint venture or a contract with someone with whom you can pool your resources and finances.

Personally your intimate relationship will become further intensified because Venus, moving through the zone of sexuality, indicates a deeper, longer-lasting bond with your partner and certainly much more sensuality. Your union with them can strengthen at this time.

Your key word after the 17th is compromise. You have to be prepared to discard the differences in styles and philosophies between yourself and others if you are to get along with them.

Making sacrifices will have to come first, before your own desires. If there have been longstanding tensions in your relationship, it's time to speak up now or forever hold your peace. Don't let arguments, particularlyover past matters, get in the road of healthy, open communication.

On the topic of sacrifice, there may be a situation that occurs for some Sagittarians during August that could be rather burdensome. You could find there are some unreasonable demands being placed on you by family members, particularly those who are older.

You may need to take care of them now and this could leave you feeling a little weary. You have to be flexible, and the planets are quite likely going to test you to see how well you handle your domestic responsibilities. You need to decompress the situation rather than making matters worse.

At times in life there's no way out of a situation and you simply have to grin and bear it. Your independent pursuits may need to take a backseat to other personal obligations.

Between the 18th and the 22nd there is an opportunity for you to connect with someone who can act as a mentor, not just practically but spiritually and emotionally as well. This is a period of renewed growth in your life and you'll begin to get someone else's spin on a situation.

It's not a bad idea to get an independent appraisal of where you're at in life and, if you're open enough, this person's aged experience, wisdom and method of communication will appeal to you and can help to unravel some of your life's mysteries.

The hard aspect of Mars and Saturn influencing your zone of friendships on the 25th could be a difficult one for you to deal with. You're best to lay low, stay out of the limelight, and let your friends deal with their own problems. Don't come between others.

Romance and friendship

Between the 1st and the 8th of August, speak up about where you want your relationship to go. There could be some tension between you and your significant other if one of you knows exactly where the relationship is going but the other feels it is still somewhat undefined.

On the 9th and the 10th you may wish to visit an old stomping ground; perhaps go to see some family members or friends and just revisit places where you used to spend time in the past. A little nostalgia will be desired by you.

From the 12th to the 18th you and your partner may not be able to come to a rational decision about something. You could be relying on each other's help to get out of a ditch, but it's best to hold off making a decision completely until you are both in a better state of mind.

You feel wildly confident about your sexual and social prowess between the 19th and the 23rd. During this phase your confidence reaches a peak and I'm pleased to say your self-esteem also is at a new high. Use these energies wisely because you shouldn't have too much trouble making friends and/or developing your existing relationships.

On the 25th and the 26th, don't put words into another person's mouth. It could be the cause of an argument. Step back and listen to what is being said. When I say 'listen', I mean listen with your heart as well as your ears.

On the 30th someone could re-open an old wound that is likely to cause you some grief. Rather than retaliating, see this as a way of completely healing and resolving some past hurts.

Work and money

Between and the 2nd and the 5th of August you may find yourself continuously discovering last-minute jobs that need to be tidied up and this could encroach on your personal life. You have a lot of explaining to do because it's likely you'll want to perform your duties well and need to spend extra time at work.

A misunderstanding around the 8th can be avoided if you ask for clarity during your discussions. Don't let embarrassment or fear of looking like an idiot stop you from asking the person to repeat themselves.

Your business sense is not so good between the 10th and the 15th. You may be impulsive by spending money on some get-rich-quick scheme or a tip for an investment portfolio. The onus is on you to investigate these pieces of gossip more thoroughly, otherwise you could end up out of pocket.

From the 17th till the 22nd, any outstanding legal issues could end favourably for you. Stop sweating it out because often many of these outcomes are in the hands of lawyers or other bureaucrats. Relax.

You have a better grip on your finances between the 29th and the 30th. Be systematic in your approach and continue to put aside just a little each month for your future security.

Destiny dates

Positive: 9, 19, 20, 21, 22, 29

Negative: 1, 25, 26

Mixed: 2, 3, 4, 5, 6, 7, 8, 10, 11, 12, 13, 14, 15, 16, 17, 18, 23, 30

SEPTEMBER 2011

Highlights of the month

Your excellent work ethics bring you into powerfully positive professional opportunities this month. Those who count will notice your ability to work well with others and see you as capable of skilful productivity and diplomatic interaction with others.

The other influence of Jupiter, which is the main factor in this interpretation, is that you can feel better physically and achieve good results in your work because you are clearheaded and healthy. You're enjoying the work you're doing, which is also making a tremendous difference to your physical wellbeing.

Between the 2nd and the 8th you'll have the steadying influence of Saturn to thank for much of your productivity, and Mercury around the 6th also gives you some intuitive brilliance that can be applied to your work as well.

In all probability you'll want to share your money by supporting someone who is having a hard time right now. Apart from friends, you could be drawn towards some humanitarian aid or cause and this could be the time to give yourself a sense that you're plugging into the global village and doing something that can help the larger community as well.

You have a strong sense of self-worth this month, and your finances as well as your self-esteem are powerfully linked. By sharing your money, your knowledge and your resources generally, you'll feel as if you're a much better person within yourself.

If you have children or deal with youngsters, you'll feel much more connected to them this month. Venus influences activities associated with these types of individuals after the 17th. If you have siblings or younger members of the family, you may opt to treat them more like children rather than the relatives that they are. In any case, you'll be extending a much more nurturing attitude towards others.

The planets ruling your early childhood will have an influence on you this month, so it's important not to bury painful events under the rug. You want to develop a secure, emotional foundation for the future, so look at your early upbringing with fresh eyes and without any sort of personal bias or judgement. Look at how this has shaped your personality in positive ways, not just negatively. You and all your relationships will ultimately benefit from this new perspective.

You have a strong sense of independence this month, and could also receive some type of award or recognition for the work you're doing. Up until the 26th you'll be feeling a great deal of intellectual curiosity and will be learning many new things about your work. Even if the type of job you do has previously been somewhat mundane, you'll somehow find a way to make it more interesting.

Those of you engaged in serious business activities may have to travel, possibly even overseas. You may also find yourself connected with foreign visitors or those whose cultures are quite different from yours but who can expand your awareness of the way you do things professionally. Taking an interest in the global markets or financial opportunities offshore could also be high on your agenda.

Between the 28th and the 30th, your profits are up. Expect some additional cash flow or some unexpected money through your work activities.

Romance and friendship

On the 1st of September you'll feel a little down about not being able to be with friends; but take heart, this is a quick-moving transit and by the 3rd or the 4th you'll be in a better position to reconnect with acquaintances who will put a smile on your face.

Between the 5th and the 7th you will feel great about yourself. Venus and the Sun bless you with popularity and a chance to make a lasting impression on some new people you meet.

There is an engagement, a birth or wedding you may be invited to during this phase of the year.

Family affairs are strongly highlighted between the 9th and the 15th, at which point, the full Moon in your zone of domestic affairs shines forth and fully activates your feeling of love. You'll also feel a stronger sense of nurturing and will want to care for people around you more than usual.

Be careful of what you say between the 23rd and the 26th. You could be revealing way too much and in the end may betray a confidence.

You're optimistic with your partner after the 27th, but this could simply highlight just how lacking in confidence the other person is. Do try to lift their spirits, but be mindful of the fact that, if you're looking big, they may be looking small.

These events continue up till the 28th or the 29th, when you should avoid the tendency of subtly coercing each other into believing, seeing or understanding things as the other does.

On the surface, things seem quite rosy between the 29th and the 30th; but below the surface, there can be tension that may create an uneasy feeling between you.

Work and money

You and a friend may have a similar problem financially and it will be a perfect opportunity around the 3rd of September to discuss these matters. You'll help yourself and others to solve this issue.

Business expenses could be irritating but necessary between the 5th and the 8th. This is unavoidable and, if you find yourself short, it simply means you haven't budgeted well enough.

After the 11th you might be pleased to learn that a lot of the money you paid in taxes may be coming back to you through some good management by a financial advisor or tax agent.

Venus moving through your zone of profits is an excellent omen for increased salary and an additional bonus, particularly if you happen to be in sales and work through a commission structure.

If you are in doubt about an investment between the 17th and the 28th, it's best to let it go. Issues surrounding money could be cloudy and you need to be sure of what you want rather than just acting on a knee jerk reaction.

Destiny dates

Positive: 2, 3, 4, 9, 10, 11, 12, 13, 14, 15

Negative: 1

Mixed: 5, 6, 7, 8, 17, 18, 19, 20, 21, 22, 23, 24, 26, 27, 28, 29, 30

OCTOBER
2011

Highlights of the month

Although you'll be feeling socially gregarious, there is considerable tension surrounding your friendships throughout the month of October. The Sun, Mercury, Saturn and Venus promise an intense and hectic social schedule.

You will be burning the candle at both ends, and this is shown by the difficult aspect between Mars and Jupiter. Between the 3rd and the 9th, especially, you need to take stock of yourself and not promise what you can't deliver.

As a flow on from this aspect, Venus does provide you with a chance to appreciate the beautiful things in life as well as be appreciated for your own personal and inner beauty. You could find yourself in the limelight this month, particularly with your superiors in your workplace.

Venus continues to dominate your life up until the end of the month, but after about the 12th there may be an opportunity for you to reconnect with someone from your past, where the end of your relationship might not have had the closure you felt it needed.

A chance to remedy that may now appear and you should avail yourself of it so you can move forward with a clean slate. Venus in your zone of endings reflects the past and hidden friends, showing that you could develop a much more spiritual insight into love and relationships.

From the 14th until the 20th Mercury provides you some answers to work issues, but you need to be prepared to do the hard work of investigating the facts and figures laid before you. You can't pretend you understand a subject, especially if you have important meetings or interviews to attend.

Researching your subject would now be advantageous to you. If you're unable to deliver on the day, the meeting will not go well for you. Don't pretend if you don't understand something, and be prepared to admit that. You'll maintain your self-respect and dignity as a result of a little humility.

Around the 22nd an interest in psychology could help you uncover some hidden or behind-the-scenes aspect of a relationship or friendship. You might be surprised to learn something about a friend that previously has been hidden and, when you uncover it, it's important how you deal with this knowledge. Not playing the blame game or judging the other person is crucial in maintaining a healthy and ongoing relationship with them.

The new Moon occurs on the 27th in your zone of profession and is positive.

Romance and friendship

Between the 2nd and the 5th of October, you and a friend or partner may realise you had so much fun previously doing something that you decide to do it all over again. This will be a humorous event, but remember it could easily be something you overdo as well. Pace yourselves.

You're not likely to encounter too much friction in your discussions, even though the topic may be heavy between the 7th and the 9th. Tread carefully in your conversations and give the other person a chance to speak so they genuinely feel that you are listening to them.

The need of a friend, or a dire financial situation, may cause you to have to drop everything at a moment's notice to help with a remedy between the 10th and the 13th. Far from this being a tedious burden, you may actually enjoy the opportunity to extend a compassionate, helping hand.

Around the 15th you may suffer a hangover or regret the night before. It's probably best to take a confidant or close friend with you if you don't feel as if you can trust yourself in a rather precarious social or even sexually charged situation.

The Sun moves into the quiet zone of your horoscope after the 24th, indicating a period when you need to sit back, relax and gather your energies rather than putting yourself out there. You should take a deep breath or two, reassess your situation, and not be coerced into going out simply for the sake of it.

Making commitments between the 29th and the 31st may not be a great idea. Everything may seem on track, but there could be one or two vital pieces of information you've left out of the equation. Stop, look and listen.

Work and money

There's considerable opposition to Jupiter from Venus, Saturn, Mercury and the Sun in your zone of work throughout this month. Between the 1st and the 7th of October you need to pace yourself more slowly and know when you have reached your limits. You can't know and do everything, and attempting to do so will only slow you down in the long run.

Brainstorming is a great idea after the 8th. Pooling your resources with some of your co-workers and acting more with a team spirit will achieve the best results.

Mercury entering the quiet zone of your horoscope on the 13th means there's lots to be done behind the scenes, away from prying eyes. Quiet, studious and meticulous work will win the day.

You may be extremely busy between the 22nd and the 30th, but there will be several occasions, most notably the 23rd, 25th, 29th and 30th, when you'll be called upon to render some service or assist someone else who is having difficulty completing their own chores.

Destiny dates

Positive: 10, 11, 12, 13, 14, 16, 17, 18, 19, 20, 21, 22, 23, 24, 25, 26, 27, 28

Negative: 1, 6, 7, 9

Mixed: 2, 3, 4, 5, 8, 15, 29, 30, 31

Highlights of the month

You'll be dealing with unfulfilled desires through-out the month of November and, between the 1st and the 5th, it's critical that you don't let anger dominate your romantic landscape if you are not physically or emotionally fulfilled.

Part of your problem is that Venus and Neptune cause you to idealise certain situations, compare yourself to others, or live through some sort of dream, viewing the world through rose-coloured glasses.

This can create confusion when you try to project these ideals into a practical situation and the other person doesn't come up to your standards. Be real-istic now and understand that you too have a lot of work to do on yourself because you may not exactly be living up to your partner's ideals, either. It takes two to tango.

After the 11th, when Mars conjoins your career zone and Venus enters your Sun sign, you'll find that business and pleasure mix up quite nicely. You'll have the opportunity to network socially and capitalise on business and financial opportunities as a result.

Market yourself; put the word out there. There's no harm—even if you're not a business person—in having a business card made up that helps to identify who you are and what you do. Expanding your social circle and personal spheres of influence will be very important to you during the middle part of November.

If you've been lax with your financial management, the presence of Mars and Pluto shows that, around the 24th, you'll be ready, willing and able to make some dramatic changes to the way you spend, earn and save money. Before making a firm decision on any financial plan on the 25th, go back over your research and the information that you've collated. Run it by your partner, a friend in the know, or even a professional who can give you a second opinion on what you plan to do. Don't let a whim dictate an economic path just now.

The new Moon on the 25th is particularly pertinent to your spiritual and evolutionary development. It's at this time you need to ponder on things using a different perspective. Getting away from the hustle and bustle of your day-to-day routine and habitual lifestyle is a must.

You need to let the surface of a pond become still before you can see deeply into it. Likewise, your mind—which at the moment could be experiencing wave after wave of doubtful thoughts or even appre-hension—similarly needs to be still before you can see deeply into your own inner self.

On the 28th, Venus and Jupiter once again bring some additional good luck to you, both in and through your workplace activities.

Romance and friendship

You are probably misguided or even self-deluded between the 1st and the 4th of November. Neptune and Venus indicate that you're putting someone on a pedestal and not realistically appraising their true worth. The character of another cannot be gauged simply over a one-hour dinner engagement. Don't be rash in assessing the true personality of a person until you've given yourself a bit more time.

The entry of Mars into the upper part of your horoscope indicates clashes with authority figures, perhaps older family members, after the 6th. Around the 7th, the presence of Mars and Neptune indicate thwarted energy and your plans almost definitely will be undermined by someone more definite or controlling in your situation.

On the 10th the Sun enters a zone of rest. Your health or some of your emotional excesses may require you to lay low and recharge your batteries.

Between the 15th and the 18th you will be trying hard to redefine your personality and where you stand in the world. You could be at cross-purposes with some of your friends or may be feeling as if they've outgrown their usefulness.

On the 22nd, rely on the advice of an older, trusted friend to help you through this period. You needn't throw out the baby with the bathwater.

The solar eclipse in your Sun sign on the 25th is a powerful antidote for sloth and lack of self-awareness. Although facing the truth within yourself about how you deal with others may be difficult during this important celestial event, the end result is most certainly clarity in your understanding of relationships.

A sudden whirlwind romance between the 27th and the 30th is ill advised. Study your motives for rushing madly into an unconventional situation. This is a case of the ends *not* justifying the means.

Work and money

This month the full Moon on the 10th in your zone of death and the new Moon on the 25th in your zone of expenditure highlight the importance of looking carefully at how you are spending your money. You are confused on the 1st of November and may believe that the money you are spending is being done so wisely, but this is not the case. Tighten your belt.

Your expenses reach a peak between the 5th and the 10th. At this point, out of sheer necessity, you may have to cull your expenses and your desires.

Between the 11th and the 17th Mars and Jupiter come to your rescue. You may be able to secure a loan that consolidates some of your credit card bills. You may be able to transfer some of your debts into a zero-interest plan for an interim period, which gives you some breathing space.

Mars and Pluto are ruthless after the 24th. Put in place a well-thought-out plan to start saving money for your future. Superannuation funds may also be high on your agenda to assess and re-evaluate.

You could receive a gift or some cash bonus around the 28th.

Destiny dates

Positive: 8, 9, 10, 11, 12, 13, 14, 22, 24, 25

Negative: 1, 2, 3, 4, 27, 29, 30

Mixed: 5, 6, 7, 15, 16, 17, 18, 28

Highlights of the month

Up to now you might not have been quite able to hook yourself up to a 'new you'. However, the new Moon on the 24th of December, just before Christmas Day, hints at the fact that you may end the year with a climax after all, in terms of being able to remodel yourself, recreate a new identity and genuinely feel as if you've achieved a considerable amount throughout the year of 2011.

The preceding full Moon on the 10th occurs in Gemini, which is your zone of marriage, and this too shows that there is a culmination of energies relating to your personal relationships. The full Moon is linked to emotional fullness and is usually considered a bright, shining and emotionally charged astrological event. On or about the same time you'll find the Venus–Mars energy bringing lots of passion, zest and sizzle to your relationships, particularly in the physical dimension.

Mercury goes forward on the 14th, indicating a clear-headed approach to your practical affairs over Christmas. Close off any paths that have only been half-travelled and you'll feel so much better, particularly by the 21st, when Venus prompts you to move out of your normal routine and to enjoy some sights and sounds out of your usual environment.

On the same day, Venus, at a right angle to Jupiter, shows that you may overdo things. Leave yourself enough time to get from one appointment to another; moderate your eating and drinking, and don't say too much. Excessive lifestyle habits could punch a hole in your energy levels leading up to Christmas.

December is usually important for Sagittarians because the Sun transits your zone of money. Try to be more frugal by spending a little less on gifts. A last-minute dash to the mall or shopping centre could find you spending way more than you had anticipated. Budget and plan this year before spending too much. Remember, it's the thought that really does count.

Christmas should be rather exciting this year, with the Sun and Uranus and also Pluto having a primary influence on your activities between the 23rd and the 29th. There are some rather scatty energies associated with Uranus. This is Christmas, after all! In your case, however, this frenetic vibe could be accentuated and you need to take a few deep breaths before rushing out madly to all those social engagements, cocktail parties and other festive routines.

A breakthrough is likely on the 29th when the Sun conjoins Pluto in your zone of finance and material values. You'll find yourself in a position of deep understanding, ready to transform yourself for the commencement of a new year.

Eliminating waste and other useless things from your life will create the space you need to attract success throughout 2012. With 2011 now complete, you're ready to continue transforming yourself by moving forward and capitalising on some of your newfound talents.

Romance and friendship

You dominate your social affairs due to the high-placed position of Mars in your horoscope in December. Over the 2nd and the 3rd you are irascible and could be quite outspoken, particularly to female members of your family. Curb your desire to be right at all costs.

Some problems associated with children—perhaps your own or other people's—between the 5th and the 7th could be time consuming and detrimental to your own peace of mind. Don't be too emotional about how you help others sort out their problems. Your example is their best teacher, remember that.

Friendships are settled between the 11th and the 20th. You can rejoice in the solidity of your bonds and the loyalty of your friends to you, and you to them.

Travels are extensive between the 21st and the 23rd and may be hectic. Make sure you plan it so that your work and social activities function harmoniously with each other leading up to Christmas.

Venus and Uranus are excellently placed between the 24th and the 26th and offer you a last-minute dose of fun in your love life. Extend that into the Christmas period because you will have a strong and attractive aura that brings some bubbly fun to the festive events in which you participate.

On the 23rd you may forget that money is a factor when you want to show your love by buying gifts. Continue to keep a rein on your spending.

You could be outlandish in the way you express yourself on the 27th. If you have a little too much to drink at that social get-together, it could be fun at the time but you may feel a little embarrassed later after you hear someone repeat what you said. Moderation is your key word in the last few days of December.

Work and money

You have to take a pre-emptive stand when it comes to bad press or some negative opinions about you in the marketplace or within your immediate workplace circle. Try to nip rumours in the bud between the 1st and the 8th, because your long-term reputation will depend on it.

The lunar eclipse on the 11th highlights the fact that you must seem to be more genuine towards your customers, particularly if you're working closely with the general public. Others are able to see through any pretence. Be genuine in your business dealings with everyone in the last few weeks of 2011.

Your debts need to be consolidated between the 21st and the 25th, even though you may rack up a few bills on those Christmas presents. Be moderate in the way you spend by remembering how more valuable your thoughts are instead of the price tag.

Jupiter moves direct on the 26th of December, highlighting your ability to feel confident that you have your debts and your finances in hand going into the beginning of 2012. Good luck, Sagittarius!

Destiny dates

Positive: 10, 11, 12, 13, 14, 15, 16, 17, 18, 19, 20

Negative: None

Mixed: 1, 2, 3, 4, 5, 6, 7, 8, 21, 22, 23, 24, 25, 26, 27, 28, 29

2011:
Astronumerology

Every man has in himslef a continent of undiscovered character. Happy is he who acts as the Columbus to his own soul.

—Sir J. Stephen

The power behind your name

It's hard to believe that your name resonates with a numerical vibration, but it's true! By simply adding the numbers of your name, you can see which planet rules you and what effects your name will have on your life and destiny. According to the ancient Chaldean system of numerology, each number is assigned a planetary energy. Take a look at the chart below to see how each alphabetical letter is connected to a planetary energy:

AIQJY	=	1	Sun
BKR	=	2	Moon
CGLS	=	3	Jupiter
DMT	=	4	Uranus
EHNX	=	5	Mercury
UVW	=	6	Venus
OZ	=	7	Neptune
FP	=	8	Saturn
—	=	9	Mars

The number 9 is not allotted a letter because it is considered 'unknowable'. Once the numbers have been added, establish which single planet rules your name and personal affairs. At this point the number 9 can be used for interpretation. Do you think it's unusual that many famous actors, writers and musicians have modified their names? This is to attract luck and good fortune, which can be made easier by using the energies of a friendlier planet. Try experimenting with the table and see how new names affect you. It's so much fun, and you may even attract greater love, wealth and worldly success!

Look at the following example to work out the power of your name. A person named Andrew Brown would calculate his ruling planet by correlating each letter to a number in the table, like this:

A N D R E W B R O W N
1 5 4 2 5 6 2 2 7 6 5

Now add the numbers like this:

1 + 5 + 4 + 2 + 5 + 6 + 2 + 2 + 7 + 6 + 5 = 45

Then add 4 + 5 = 9

The ruling number of Andrew Brown's name is 9, which is ruled by Mars (see how the 9 can now be used?). Now study the name–number table to reveal the power of your name. The numbers 4 and 5 will also play a secondary role in Andrew's character and destiny, so in this case you would also study the effects of Uranus (4) and Mercury (5).

Name–number table

Your name-number	Ruling planet	Your name characteristics
1	**Sun**	Attractive personality. Magnetic charm. Superman-, superwoman-like vitality and physical energy. Incredibly active and gregarious. Enjoys outdoor activities and sports. Has friends and individuals in powerful positions. Good government connections. Intelligent, spectacular, flashy and successful. A loyal number for love and relationships.
2	**Moon**	Feminine and soft, emotional temperament. Fluctuating moods but intuitive, and possibly even clairvoyant abilities. Ingenious nature and kind-hearted expression of feelings. Loves family, mothering and home life. Night owl who probably needs more sleep. Success with the public and/or women generally.
3	**Jupiter**	Sociable, optimistic number with fortunate destiny. Attracts opportunities without too much effort. Great sense of timing. Religious or spiritual inclinations. Naturally drawn to investigate the meaning of life. Philosophical insight. Enjoys travel and to explore the world and different cultures.
4	**Uranus**	Volatile character with many peculiar aspects. Likes to experiment and test novel experiences. Forward thinking, with many extraordinary friends. Gets bored easily so needs plenty of inspiring activities. Pioneering, technological and creative. Wilful and obstinate at times. Unforeseen events in life may be positive or negative.

Your name-number	Ruling planet	Your name characteristics
5	Mercury	Sharp wit, quick thinking and with great powers of speech. Extremely active life. Always on the go, living on nervous energy. Youthful outlook and never grows old. Looks younger than actual age. Young friends and humorous disposition. Loves reading and writing. Great communicator.
6	Venus	Delightful and charming. Graceful and eye-catching personality who cherishes and nourishes friends. Very active social life. Musical or creative interests. Great moneymaking opportunities as well as numerous love affairs indicated. Career in the public eye is quite likely. Loves family but is often troubled over divided loyalties with friends.
7	Neptune	Intuitive, spiritual and self-sacrificing nature. Easily duped by those who need help. Loves to dream of life's possibilities. Has healing powers. Dreams are revealing and prophetic. Loves water and will have many journeys in life. Spiritual aspirations dominate worldly desires.
8	Saturn	Hard-working, ambitious person with slow yet certain achievements. Remarkable concentration and self-sacrifice for a chosen objective. Financially focused but generous when a person's trust is gained. Proficient in one's chosen field but is a hard taskmaster. Demands perfection and needs to relax and enjoy life.

Your name-number	Ruling planet	Your name characteristics
9	Mars	Extraordinary physical drive, desires and ambition. Sports and outdoor activities are major keys to health. Confrontational but likes to work and play really hard. Protects and defends family, friends and territory. Individual tastes in life but also self-absorbed. Needs to listen to others' advice to gain greater successes.

Your 2011 planetary ruler

Astrology and numerology are intimately connected. As already shown, each planet rules over a number between 1 and 9. Both your name *and* your birth date are governed by planetary energies.

Simply add the numbers of your birth date and the year in question to find out which planet will control the coming year for you. Here is an example:

If you were born on the 12th of November, add the numerals 1 and 2, for your day of birth, and 1 and 1, for your month of birth, to the year in question, in this case 2011, the current year, like this:

Add 1 + 2 + 1 + 1 + 2 + 0 + 1+ 1 = 9

The planet ruling your individual karma for 2011 will be Mars because this planet rules the number 9.

You can even take your ruling name-number, as shown previously, and add it to the year in question, to throw more light on your coming personal affairs, like this:

A N D R E W B R O W N = 9
Year coming = 2011
Add 9 + 2 + 0 + 1 + 1 = 13
Add 1 + 3 = 4

This is the ruling year number, using your name-number as a basis.

Therefore, study Uranus's (number 4) influence for 2011. Enjoy!

1 is the year of the Sun

Overview

The year 2011 is the commencement of a new cycle for you. Because the Sun rules the number 1, the dominant energy for you in the coming year is solar, which is also connected to the sign of Leo. Expect the coming year to be full of great accomplishments and a high reputation regarding new plans and projects. This is the turning of a new page in the book of your life.

You will experience an uplifting of your physical energies, which makes you ready to assume fresh responsibilities in a new nine-year cycle. Whatever you begin now will surely be successful.

Your physical vitality is strong and your health should improve. If you've been suffering physical ailments, this is the time to improve your physical wellbeing because recovery will be certain.

You're a magnetic person this year, so attracting people into your life won't be difficult. Expect a new circle of friends and possibly even new lovers coming into your life. Get ready to be invited to many parties and different engagements. However, don't go burning the midnight oil because this will overstretch your physical powers.

Don't be too cocky with friends or employers. Maintain some humility, which will make you even more popular throughout 2011.

Love and pleasure

Because this is the commencement of a new cycle, you'll be lucky in love. The Sun also has influence over children, so your family life will also entail more responsibility. Music, art and any other creative activities will be high on your agenda and may be the source of a new romance for you.

Work

Because you are so popular and powerful this year, you won't need to exert too much effort to attract luck, money and new windows of opportunity through your work and group activities. Changes that you make professionally now will pay off, particularly in the coming couple of years. Promotions are likely and don't be surprised to see some extra money coming your way as a pay rise.

Improving your luck

Because Leo and the number 1 are your rulers this year, you'll be especially lucky without too much effort. The months of July and August, being ruled by Leo, are very lucky for you. The 1st, 8th, 15th and 22nd hours of Sundays will be especially lucky. You may also find yourself meeting Leos and they may be able to contribute something to your good fortune throughout the coming year.

This year your lucky numbers are 1, 10, 19 and 28.

2 is the year of the Moon

Overview

The Moon represents emotional, nurturing, mothering and feminine aspects of our natures and 2011 will embody all of these traits in you, and more.

Groundbreaking opportunities in your relationships with family members can be expected. This will offer you immense satisfaction.

Your emotional and mental moods and habits should be examined. If you are reactive in your life, this year will be the perfect time to take greater control of yourself. The sign of Cancer, which is ruled by the Moon, is also very much linked to the number 2 and therefore people born under this sign may have an important role to play in your life.

Love and pleasure

Your home, family life and interpersonal relationships will be the main arenas of activity for you in 2011. You'll be able to take your relationships to a new level. If you haven't had the time to dedicate and devote yourself to the people you love, you can do so throughout the coming twelve months.

Thinking of moving? These lunar energies may cause you to change your residence or renovate your current home to make your living circumstances much more in tune with your mind and your heart.

Work

Working from home can be a great idea—or at least, spending more time alone to focus your attention on what you really want—will benefit you professionally. You need to control yourself and think carefully about how you are going to achieve your desired goals.

Women can be a source of opportunity for you and, if you're looking for a change in work, use your connections, especially feminine ones, to achieve success.

Improving your luck

The sign of Cancer being ruled by the Moon also has a connection with Mondays and therefore this will be one of your luckier days throughout 2011. The month of July is also one in which some of your dreams may come true. The 1st, 8th, 15th and 22nd hours on Mondays are successful times. Pay special attention to the new and full Moons in 2011.

The numbers 2, 11, 20, 29 and 38 are lucky for you.

3 is the year of Jupiter

Overview

Number 3 is one of the luckiest numbers, being ruled by Jupiter. Therefore, 2011 should be an exciting and expansive year for you. The planet Jupiter and the sign of Sagittarius will dominate the affairs of your life.

Under the number 3 you'll desire a richer, deeper and broader experience of life and as a result your horizons will also be much broader. You have the ability to gain money, to increase your popularity, and to have loads of fun.

Generosity is one of the key words of the number 3 and you're likely to help others fulfil their desires, too. There is an element of humanity and self-sacrifice indicated by this number and so the more spiritual and compassionate elements of your personality will bubble to the surface. You can improve yourself as a person generally, and this is also a year when your good karma should be used unselfishly to help others as well as yourself.

Love and pleasure

Exploring the world through travel will be an important component of your social and romantic life throughout 2011. It's quite likely that, through your travels and your contacts in other places, you may meet people who will spur you on to love and romance.

You'll be a bit of a gambler in 2011 and the number 3 will make you speculative. This could mean a few false starts in the area of love, but don't be afraid to explore the signs of human possibilities. You may just meet your soulmate as a result.

If you're currently in a relationship, you can deepen your love for each other and push the relationship to new heights.

Work

This is a fortunate year for you. The year 2011 brings you opportunities and success. Your employers will listen to your ideas and accommodate your requests for extra money.

Starting a new job is likely, possibly even your own business. You will try something big and bold. Have no fear: success is on your side.

Improving your luck

As long as you don't push yourself too hard you will have a successful year. Maintain a first-class plan and stick to it. Be realistic about what you are capable of. On the 1st, 8th, 15th and 24th hours of Thursdays, your intuition will make you lucky.

Your lucky numbers this year are 3, 12, 21 and 30. March and December are lucky months. The year 2011 will bring you some unexpected surprises.

4 is the year of Uranus
Overview

Expect the unexpected in 2011. This is a year when you achieve extraordinary things but have to make serious choices between several opportunities. You need to break free of your own past self-limitations, off-load any baggage that is hindering you, in both your personal and professional lives. It's an independent year and self-development will be important to achieving success.

Discipline is one of your key words for 2011. Maintain an orderly lifestyle, a clear-cut routine, and get more sleep. You'll gain strong momentum to fulfil yourself in each and every department of your life.

Love and pleasure

You may be dissatisfied with the current status quo in your relationships, so you're likely to break free and experiment with something different. Your relationships will be anything but dull or routine. You're looking for someone who is prepared to explore emotional and sexual landscapes.

Your social life will also be exciting and you'll meet unusual people who will open your eyes to new and fruitful activities. Spiritual and self-help activities will also capture your attention and enable you to make the most of your new friendships.

Work

The number 4 is modern, progressive and ruled by Uranus. Due to this, all sorts of technological gadgets, computing and Internet activities will play a significant role in your professional life. Move ahead with the times and upgrade your professional skills, because any new job you attempt will require it.

Work could be a little overwhelming, especially if you've not been accustomed to keeping a tight schedule. Be more efficient with your time.

Groups are important to your work efforts this year, so utilise your friends in finding a position you desire. Listen to their advice and become more of a team player because this will be a short cut in your pathway to success.

Improving your luck

Slow your pace this year because being impulsive will only cause you to make errors and waste time. 'Patience is a virtue', but in your case, when being ruled by the number 4, patience will be even more important for you.

The 1st, 8th, 15th and 20th hours of any Saturday will be very lucky for you in 2011.

Your lucky numbers are 4, 13, 22 and 31.

5 is the year of Mercury

Overview

Owing to the rulership of 2011 by the number 5, your intellectual and communicative abilities will be at a peak. Your imagination is also greatly stimulated by Mercury and so exciting new ideas will be constantly churning in your mind.

The downside of the number 5 is its convertible nature, which means it's likely that, when crunch times come and you have to make decisions, it will be difficult to do so. Get all your information together before drawing a firm conclusion. Develop a strong will and unshakable attitude to overcome distractions.

Contracts, new job offers and other agreements also need to be studied carefully before coming to any decision. Business skills and communication are the key words for your life in 2011.

Love and pleasure

One of the contributing factors to your love life in 2011 is service. You must learn to give to your partner if you wish to receive. There may be a change in your routine and this will be necessary if you are to keep your love life exciting, fresh and alive.

You could be critical, so be careful if you are trying to correct the behaviour of others. You'll be blunt and this will alienate you from your peers. Maintain some control over your critical mind before handing out your opinions.

You are likely to become interested in beautifying yourself and looking your best.

Work

Your ideas will be at the forefront of your professional activities this year. You are fast, capable and also innovative in the way you conduct yourself in the workplace. If you need to make any serious changes, however, it is best to think twice before jumping out of the pan and into the fire.

Travel will also be a big component of your working life this year, and you can expect a hectic schedule with lots of flitting about here, there and everywhere. Pace yourself.

Improving your luck

Your greatest fortune will be in communicating ideas. Don't jump from one idea to another too quickly, though, because this will dilute your success.

Listen to your body signals as well because your health is strongly governed by the number 5. Sleep well, eat sensibly and exercise regularly to rebuild your resilience and strength.

The 1st, 8th, 15th and 20th hours of Wednesdays are your luckiest, so schedule your meetings and other important social engagements at these times.

Throughout 2011 your lucky numbers are 5, 14, 23 and 32.

6 is the year of Venus

Overview

The number 6 can be summed up in one beautiful four-letter word: LOVE! Venus rules 6 and is well known for its sensual, romantic and marital overtones. The year 2011 offers you all of this and more. If you're looking for a soulmate, it's likely to happen under a 6 vibration.

This year is a period of hard work to improve your security and finances. Saving money, cutting costs and looking to your future will be important. Keep in mind that this is a year of sharing love *and* material resources.

Love and pleasure

Romance is a key feature of 2011 and, if you're currently in a relationship, you can expect it to become more fulfilling. Important karmic connections are likely during this 6 year for those of you who are not yet married or in a relationship.

Beautify yourself, get a new hairstyle, work on looking your best through improving your fashion sense, new styles of jewellery and getting out there and showing the world what you're made of. This is a year in which your social engagements result in better relationships.

Try not to overdo it, because Venus has a tendency towards excess. Moderation in all things is important in a Venus year 6.

Work

The year 2011 will stimulate your knowledge about finance and your future security. You'll be capable of cutting back expenses and learning how to stretch a dollar. There could be surplus cash this year, increased income or some additional bonuses. You'll use this money to improve your living circumstances because home life is also important under a 6 year.

Your domestic situation could also be tied in with your work. During this year of Venus, your business and social activities will overlap.

Improving your luck

Money will flow as long as you keep an open mind and positive attitude. Remove negative personality traits obstructing you from greater luck. Be moderate in your actions and don't focus primarily on money. Your spiritual needs also require attention.

The 1st, 8th, 15th and 20th hours on Fridays are extremely lucky for you this year and new opportunities can arise when you least expect it.

The numbers 6, 15, 24 and 33 will generally increase your luck.

7 is the year of Neptune

Overview

Under a 7 year of Neptune, your spiritual and intuitive powers peak. Although your ideals seem clearer and more spiritually orientated, others may not understand your purpose. Develop the power of your convictions to balance your inner ideals with the practical demands of life.

You must learn to let go of your past emotional issues, break through these barriers to improve your life and your relationships this year. This might require you to sever ties with some of the usual people you have become accustomed to being with, which will give you the chance to focus on your own inner needs.

Love and pleasure

Relationships may be demanding and it's at this point in your life that you'll realise you have to give something to yourself as well, not just give to others indefinitely. If the people that matter most in your life are not reciprocating and meeting your needs, you'll have to make some important changes this year.

When it comes to helping others, pick your mark. Not everyone is deserving of the love and resources you have to offer. If you're indiscriminate, you could find yourself with egg on your face if you have been taken advantage of. Be firm, but compassionate.

Work

Compassionate work best describes 2011 under a 7 year. But the challenges of your professional life give you greater insight into yourself and the ability to see clearly what you *don't* want in your life any more. Remove what is unnecessary and this will pave the way for brighter successes.

Caring for and helping others will be important because your work will now bring you to a point where you realise that selfishness, money and security are not the only important things in life. Helping others will be part of your process, which will bring excellent benefits.

Improving your luck

Self-sacrifice, along with discipline and personal discrimination, bring luck. Don't let people use you because this will only result in more emotional baggage. The law of karma states that what you give, you will receive in greater measure; but sometimes the more you give, the more people take, too. Remember that.

The 1st, 8th, 15th and 20th hours of Tuesdays will be lucky times this year.

Try the numbers 7, 16, 25 and 34 to increase your luck.

8 is the year of Saturn

Overview

The number 8 is the most practical of the numbers, being ruled by Saturn and Capricorn. This means that your discipline, attention to detail and hard work will help you achieve your goals. Remaining solitary and not being overly involved with people will help you focus on things that matter. Resisting temptation will be part of your challenge this year, but doing so will also help you become a better person.

Love and pleasure

Balance your personal affairs with work. If you pay too much attention to your work, finances and your professional esteem, you may be missing out on the simple things in life, mainly love and affection.

Being responsible is certainly a great way to show your love to the ones who matter to you, such as your family members. But if you're concerned only with work and no play, it makes for a very dull family life. Make a little more time to enjoy your family and friends and schedule some time off on the weekends so you can enjoy the journey, not just the goal.

Work

You can make a lot of money this year and, if you've been focused on your work for the last couple of years, this is a time when money should flow to you. The Chinese believe the number 8 is indeed the money number and can bring you the fruits of your hard labour.

Because you're cautious and resourceful you'll be able to save more this year, but try not to be too stingy with your money.

Under an 8 year you'll take on new responsibilities. You mustn't do this for the sake of looking good. If you truly like the work that is being offered, by all means take it. But if it's simply for the sake of ego, you'll be very disappointed.

Improving your luck

This year you could be a little reluctant to try new things. But if you are overly cautious, you may miss opportunities. Don't act impulsively on what is being offered, of course, but do be open to trying some alternative things as well.

Be gentle and kind to yourself. By pampering yourself you send out a strong signal to the universe that you are deserving of some rewards.

The 1st, 8th, 15th and 20th hours of Saturdays are the best times for you in 2011.

The numbers 1, 8, 17, 26 and 35 are your lucky numbers.

9 is the year of Mars
Overview

The year 2011 is the final year of a nine-year cycle and this will be dominated by Aries and Mars. You'll be rushing madly to complete many things, so be careful not to overstep the mark of your capability. Work hard but balance your life with adequate rest.

In your relationships you will realise that you are at odds with your partner and want different things. This is the time to talk it out. If the communication between you isn't flowing well, you might find yourself leaving the relationship and moving on to bigger or better things. Worthwhile communication is a two-way street that will benefit both of you.

Love and pleasure

Mars is very pushy and infuses the number 9 with this kind of energy. The upshot is you need to be gentle in conveying your ideas and offering your views. Avoid arguments if you want to improve your relationships.

If you feel it's time for a change, discuss it with your partner. You can work through this feeling together and create an exciting new pathway for your love life. Don't get too angry with the little things in life. Get out and play some sport if you feel you are inappropriately taking out your bad moods on the ones you love.

Work

You have an intense drive and strong capability to achieve anything you choose in 2011. But be careful you don't overdo things, because you are prone to pushing yourself too far. Pace your deadlines, stagger the workload and, if possible, delegate some of the more menial tasks to others so you'll have time to do your own work properly.

Number 9 has an element of leadership associated with it, so you may be asked to take over and lead the group. This brings with it added responsibility but can also inspire you greatly.

Improving your luck

Restlessness is one of the problems that the number 9 brings with it, so you must learn to meditate and pacify your mind so you can take advantage of what the universe has to offer. If you're scattered in your energies, your attention will miss vital opportunities and your relationships could also become rather problematic as well.

Your health and vitality will remain strong as long as you rest adequately and find suitable outlets for your tension.

The 1st, 8th, 15th and 20th hours of Tuesdays will be lucky for you throughout 2011. Your lucky numbers are 9, 18, 27 and 36.

SAGITTARIUS

2011:
Your Daily Planner

We are what we repeatedly do. Excellence, therefore, is not an act but a habit.

— Aristotle

There is a little-known branch of astrology called electional astrology, and it can help you select the most appropriate times for many of your day-to-day activities.

Ancient astrologers understood the planetary patterns and how they impacted on each of us. This allowed them to suggest the best possible times to start various important activities. Many farmers today still use this approach: they understand the phases of the Moon, and attest to the fact that planting seeds on certain lunar days produces a far better crop than planting on other days.

The following section covers many areas of day-to-day life, and uses the cycles of the Moon and the combined strength of the other planets to work out the best times to start different types of activity.

So to create your own personal almanac, first select the activity you are interested in, then quickly scan the year for the best months to start it. When you have selected the month, you can finetune your timing by finding the best specific dates. You can then be sure that the planetary energies will be in sync with you, offering you the best possible outcome.

Coupled with what you know about your monthly and weekly trends, the daily planner can be a powerful tool to help you capitalise on opportunities that come your way this year.

Good luck, and may the planets bless you with great success, fortune and happiness in 2011!

Starting activities

How many times have you made a new year's resolution to begin a diet or be a better person in your relationships? And how many times has it not worked out? Well, part of the reason may be that you started out at the wrong time, because how successful you are is strongly influenced by the position of the Moon and the planets when you begin a particular activity. You will be more successful with the following endeavours if you start them on the days indicated.

Relationships

We all feel more empowered on some days than on others. This is because the planets have some power over us—their movement and their relationships to each other determine the ebb and flow of our energies. And our level of self-confidence and our sense of romantic magnetism play an important part in the way we behave in relationships.

Your daily planner tells you the ideal dates for meeting new friends, initiating a love affair, spending time with family and loved ones—it even tells you the most appropriate times for sexual encounters.

You'll be surprised at how much more impact you can make in your relationships when you tune yourself in to the planetary energies on these special dates.

Falling in love or restoring love

During these times you could expect favourable energies to be present to meet your soulmate. Or, if you've had difficulty in a relationship, you can approach the one you love to rekindle both your and their emotional responses.

January	8, 9, 10, 13, 14, 15, 18, 19, 20, 21
February	4, 5, 6, 9, 10, 11, 14
March	1, 9, 10, 14, 15, 16, 17
April	5, 6, 17, 25, 26
May	3, 4, 6, 7, 8, 9, 10, 11, 14, 15, 22, 23, 24
June	1, 11, 18, 19, 20, 28, 29, 30
July	7, 8, 26, 27, 30, 31
August	3, 12, 13, 14, 22, 23, 27, 31
September	1, 18, 19, 20, 26, 27, 28, 29, 30
October	12, 13, 17, 18, 25, 26, 29, 30, 31
November	2, 3, 4, 5, 6, 9, 17, 29
December	3, 7, 8, 11, 14, 15, 18, 19, 29, 30

Special times with friends and family

Socialising, partying and having a good time with those you enjoy being with is highly favourable under the following dates. These are also excellent days to spend time with family and loved ones in a domestic environment:

January	17, 20, 21
February	2, 9, 10, 11, 18, 19, 20, 21, 22, 23, 24, 28
March	1, 11, 14, 16, 17, 20
April	2, 11, 12, 21, 22, 26
May	6, 9, 10, 11, 14, 15, 22, 23, 24
June	4, 8, 10, 12, 19, 20, 25, 26, 28
July	7, 8, 16, 23, 30, 31
August	4, 5, 6, 7, 13, 20, 27, 31
September	1, 6, 18, 19, 20, 29, 30
October	1, 16, 17, 25, 26
November	2, 12, 13, 17, 26, 29
December	11, 14, 15, 18, 19, 27, 28

Healing or resuming a relationship

If you're trying to get back together with the one you love and need a heart-to-heart or deep and meaningful conversation, you can try the following dates to do so:

January	2, 3, 4, 5, 6, 7, 8, 9, 10, 11, 12, 13, 14, 15, 16, 17, 18, 19, 20, 21, 28
February	1, 2, 4, 5, 6, 7, 21, 22, 23, 24, 28
March	1, 8, 9, 10, 11, 14, 16, 17, 18, 19, 20
April	2, 11, 12, 26

May	1, 6, 7, 8, 9, 10, 11, 12, 13, 15, 19, 22, 24, 25, 26, 27, 28
June	5, 12, 14, 15, 16, 19, 23, 25, 26, 27, 28, 29, 30
July	4, 6, 7, 8, 9, 10, 16, 19, 21, 23, 28, 29, 30, 31
August	1, 2, 3, 13, 15, 16, 20, 27, 29, 30, 31
September	1, 2, 3, 4, 5, 6, 13, 15, 16, 17, 18, 19, 20, 21, 22, 23, 25, 28, 29
October	12, 13, 15, 16, 17, 18, 25, 27, 29
November	2, 4, 5, 6, 15, 16, 17, 26, 29
December	11, 19, 20, 21, 22, 23

Sexual encounters

Physical and sexual energies are well favoured on the following dates. The energies of the planets enhance your moments of intimacy during these times:

January	2, 3, 4, 5, 6, 7, 8, 9, 10, 11, 12, 20, 21, 25
February	7, 8, 18, 19, 20, 21
March	1, 8, 11, 14, 20, 21
April	4, 11, 12, 25, 26, 27, 28, 29
May	2, 9, 10, 11, 14, 15, 22, 23, 24
June	1, 11, 12, 18, 19, 20, 28, 29, 30

July	7, 8, 16, 19, 20, 21, 23, 30
August	3, 12, 13, 14, 20, 22, 27, 31
September	1, 18, 19, 20, 29, 30
October	1, 13, 15, 18, 19, 20, 21, 22, 25, 26
November	2, 3, 11, 15, 16, 17, 18, 21, 22
December	5, 6, 12, 13, 14, 15, 18, 19

Health and wellbeing

Your aura and life force are susceptible to the movements of the planets; in particular, they respond to the phases of the Moon.

The following dates are the most appropriate times to begin a diet, have cosmetic surgery, or seek medical advice. They also tell you when the best times are to help others.

Feeling of wellbeing

Your physical as well as your mental alertness should be strong on these following dates. You can plan your activities and expect a good response from others:

January	7, 9, 10, 11, 12, 13, 14, 18, 20, 21
February	4, 18, 19, 20, 21, 22, 23, 24
March	16, 17, 19, 20
April	2, 7, 12, 20, 22, 25, 26
May	9, 10, 11, 14, 15, 16, 17, 22, 24, 25

June	4, 8, 10, 11, 12, 16, 17, 18, 19, 20, 21, 23, 25, 26
July	7, 8, 9, 10, 26, 27, 30
August	3, 4, 5, 6, 12, 13, 14, 17, 19, 22, 27, 31
September	1, 13, 26, 27, 28, 29, 30
October	1, 16, 17, 25, 26, 30, 31
November	1, 2, 3, 4, 5, 6, 17, 29
December	4, 11, 14, 15, 18, 19, 21, 22, 23, 30

Healing and medical

These times are good for approaching others who have expertise when you need some deeper understanding. They are also favourable for any sort of healing or medication, and for making appointments with doctors or psychologists. Planning surgery around these dates should bring good results.

Often giving up our time and energy to assist others doesn't necessarily result in the expected outcome. By lending a helping hand to a friend on the following dates, the results should be favourable:

January	1, 2, 3, 4, 5, 6, 7, 8, 14, 15, 16, 17, 18, 19, 20, 21, 22, 23, 24, 25, 26, 27, 28, 29, 31
February	3, 4, 5, 6, 7, 8, 9, 10, 13, 15, 16, 17, 18, 19, 21, 22, 23, 24, 25, 26, 27
March	4, 9, 10, 11, 12, 15, 16

April	2, 9, 10, 11, 12, 13, 14, 15, 16, 17, 18, 19, 20, 21, 22, 23, 24, 25, 26, 27, 28, 29, 30
May	1, 2, 3, 4, 5, 6, 8, 9, 10, 11, 12, 13, 14, 15, 16, 17, 18, 19, 20, 21, 22, 23, 24, 25, 30
June	23, 26, 28
July	3, 10, 11, 12
August	7, 8, 9, 10, 11, 12, 13, 14, 15, 16, 20, 21, 25
September	23, 25, 26, 27
October	20, 21, 22, 23, 24, 25, 26, 27, 28, 29, 30, 31
November	1, 2, 3, 4, 5, 6, 7, 8, 9, 10, 11, 12, 13, 14, 15, 16, 17, 18, 19, 20, 21, 22, 23, 24, 25, 30
December	1, 2, 3, 4, 5, 6, 7, 8, 9, 10, 30

Money

Money is an important part of life, and involves lots of decisions—decisions about borrowing, investing, spending. The ideal times for transactions are very much influenced by the planets, and whether your investment or nest egg grows or doesn't grow can often be linked to timing. Making your decisions on the following dates could give you a whole new perspective on your financial future:

Managing wealth and money

To build your nest egg it's a good time to open a bank account and invest money on the following dates:

January	2, 3, 9, 10, 11, 12, 13, 14, 15, 16, 17, 18, 19, 20, 21, 22, 24, 28
February	3, 4, 5, 6, 7, 8, 9, 11, 13, 14, 16, 18, 19, 20, 21, 22, 23, 24, 25, 26, 27
March	4, 8, 11, 12, 13, 14, 16, 17, 18, 19
April	2, 7, 8, 9, 10, 11, 12, 13, 16, 17, 18, 19, 20, 21, 22, 23, 24, 25
May	1, 6, 7, 8, 9, 10, 11, 12, 13, 14, 15, 16, 17, 18, 19, 20, 21, 22, 23, 24, 25, 30
June	3, 4, 5, 8, 16, 17, 18, 19, 20, 23, 25, 26, 27, 28
July	4, 5, 6, 7, 8, 9, 10, 11, 12, 16, 23, 25, 28, 29, 30, 31
August	1, 2, 3, 4, 5, 6, 7, 8, 9, 10, 11, 12, 13, 14, 15, 16, 17, 19, 20, 30, 31
September	2, 11, 13, 15, 23, 25, 26, 27, 28, 29, 30
October	1, 2, 3, 4, 5, 6, 7, 8, 13, 14, 15, 16, 17, 18, 19, 21, 24, 25, 26, 27, 28, 29, 30, 31
November	2, 3, 4, 5, 6, 7, 9, 11, 12, 13, 14, 15, 16, 17, 18, 19, 20, 23, 25, 29
December	6, 13, 19, 26, 31

Spending

It's always fun to spend, but the following dates are more in tune with this activity and are likely to give you better results:

January	8, 9, 10, 11, 12, 13, 14, 15
February	9, 11, 18, 19
March	9
April	22
May	6, 7, 8, 9, 10, 11, 12, 13, 14, 17, 18, 19, 20, 21, 22, 23, 24
June	4, 8, 10, 11, 12, 14, 16, 17, 19
July	6, 7, 8, 9, 10, 11, 31
August	1, 2, 3, 4, 5, 6, 15, 16, 17, 18, 19, 30, 31
September	1, 2, 3, 4, 17, 19, 28, 29, 30
October	12, 13, 14, 15, 16, 17, 18, 19, 27, 28, 29, 30, 31
November	2, 3, 4, 5, 6, 7
December	3, 4, 5, 22, 23

Selling

If you're thinking of selling something, whether it is small or large, consider the following dates as ideal times to do so:

January	2, 3, 9, 10, 11, 12, 13, 14, 15, 16, 17, 18, 19, 20, 22, 24, 28
February	3, 4, 5, 6, 7, 8, 9, 11, 13, 14, 16, 18, 19, 20, 21, 22, 23, 24, 25, 26, 27
March	4, 8, 11, 12, 13, 14, 16, 17, 18, 19
April	2, 7, 8, 9, 10, 11, 12, 13, 16, 17, 18, 19, 20, 21, 22, 23, 24
May	1, 6, 7, 8, 9, 10, 11, 12, 13, 14, 15, 16, 17, 18, 19, 20, 21, 22, 23, 24, 25, 26, 30
June	3, 4, 5, 8, 16, 17, 18, 19, 20, 23, 25, 26, 27, 28
July	4, 5, 6, 7, 8, 9, 10, 11, 12, 16, 23, 25, 28, 29, 30, 31
August	1, 2, 3, 4, 5, 6, 7, 8, 9, 10, 11, 12, 13, 14, 15, 16, 17, 19, 20, 30, 31
September	2, 11, 13, 15, 23, 25, 26, 27, 28, 29, 30
October	1, 2, 3, 4, 5, 6, 7, 8, 13, 14, 15, 16, 17, 18, 19, 21, 24, 25, 26, 27, 28, 29, 30, 31
November	2, 3, 4, 5, 6, 7, 9, 11, 12, 13, 14, 15, 16, 17, 18, 19, 20, 23, 25, 29
December	2, 3, 4, 5, 6, 7, 11, 30

Borrowing

Few of us like to borrow money, but if you must, taking out a loan on the following dates will be positive:

January	1, 20, 21, 26, 27, 28, 31
February	1, 2, 22, 23, 24
March	1, 22, 23, 26, 27, 29, 31
April	1, 18, 19, 22, 23, 24, 25, 26, 27, 28, 29
May	17, 18, 19, 20, 21, 22, 23, 24, 25, 26
June	16, 17, 18, 19, 22
July	15, 16, 28, 29, 30
August	15, 16, 24, 25, 26, 27, 28
September	21, 22
October	21
November	14, 15, 16, 17, 23, 24
December	12, 13, 14, 15, 20, 21, 22, 23, 24

Speculation and investment

To invest your money and get a good return on that investment, try taking a punt on the following dates:

January	3, 4, 5, 11, 12, 18, 19, 24, 25, 31
February	1, 7, 8, 14, 15, 20, 21, 27, 28
March	6, 7, 8, 14, 15, 20, 21, 26, 27
April	2, 3, 4, 10, 11, 16, 17, 22, 23, 24, 30

May	1, 7, 8, 14, 15, 20, 21, 27, 28, 29
June	3, 4, 5, 10, 11, 16, 17, 23, 24, 25
July	1, 2, 7, 8, 14, 15, 21, 22, 28, 29
August	3, 4, 10, 11, 17, 18, 19, 24, 25, 26, 31
September	1, 6, 7, 13, 14, 15, 21, 22, 27, 28
October	3, 4, 5, 11, 12, 18, 19, 25, 26, 31
November	1, 7, 8, 14, 15, 16, 21, 22, 27, 28
December	4, 5, 6, 12, 13, 18, 19, 25, 26, 31

Work and education

Your career is important to you, and continual improvement of your skills is therefore also crucial, professionally, mentally and socially. These dates will help you find out the most appropriate times to improve your professional talents and commence new work or education associated with your work.

You may need to decide when to start learning a new skill, when to ask for a promotion, and even when to make an important career change. Here are the days when your mental and educational power is strong.

Learning new skills

Educational pursuits are lucky and bring good results on the following dates:

January	16, 17
February	12, 13

March	11, 12, 13, 18, 19
April	7, 8, 9, 14, 15
May	5, 6, 12, 13
June	2, 8, 9, 14, 15
July	5, 6, 11, 12, 13
August	1, 2, 8, 9, 29, 30
September	4, 5
October	1, 2, 29, 30
November	25, 26
December	9, 10

Changing career path or profession

If you're feeling stuck and need to move into a new professional activity, changing jobs is recommended at these times:

January	4, 5, 13, 14, 15
February	9, 10, 11
March	1, 2, 3, 9, 10, 11, 12, 18, 19, 20, 21
April	5, 6, 7, 8, 9, 14, 15, 16, 17, 25, 26
May	3, 4, 12, 13, 22, 23, 24
June	1, 2, 8, 9, 18, 19, 20, 28, 29, 30
July	5, 6, 14, 26, 27
August	3, 4, 10, 11, 22, 23, 29, 30, 31
September	1, 6, 7, 8, 9, 10, 18, 19, 20, 27, 28

2011: YOUR DAILY PLANNER

October	3, 4, 5, 16, 17, 25, 26, 31
November	1, 2, 3, 9, 10, 29, 30
December	1, 7, 8, 9, 10, 11, 18, 19, 25, 26, 27, 28

Promotion, professional focus and hard work

To increase your mental focus and achieve good results from the work you do; promotions are also likely on the dates that follow:

January	3, 9, 10, 11, 12, 13, 14, 18
February	22, 23, 24, 25, 26, 27, 28
March	8, 10, 11, 13, 14, 16, 17, 18, 19
April	11, 12
May	6, 7, 8, 9, 10, 11, 12, 13, 15, 16, 17, 19, 21, 22, 23, 24
June	4, 5, 8, 11, 12, 14, 15, 16, 17, 19
July	16, 18, 19, 20, 23, 24, 25, 28, 29, 30
August	1, 2, 14, 15, 16, 17, 19, 30
September	1, 2, 3, 4, 5, 6, 11, 13, 16, 17, 19
October	13, 15, 16, 17, 18, 19
November	2, 4, 5, 6, 7, 12
December	25, 26

Travel

Setting out on a holiday or adventurous journey is exciting. Here are the most favourable times for doing this. Travel on the following dates is likely to give you a sense of fulfilment:

January	9, 10, 11, 12, 16, 17, 18, 19
February	4, 5, 6, 7, 15
March	19
April	7, 8, 9, 10, 11
May	15
June	4, 8, 10, 11
July	1, 5, 6
August	1, 2, 3, 4, 8
September	27, 28
October	1, 3, 4, 29, 30, 31
November	1, 4, 5, 6
December	3, 4, 5, 25, 29, 30

Beauty and grooming

Believe it or not, cutting your hair or nails has a powerful effect on your body's electromagnetic energy. If you cut your hair or nails at the wrong time of the month, you can reduce your level of vitality significantly. Use these dates to ensure you optimise your energy levels by staying in tune with the stars:

Haircuts

January	1, 2, 8, 9, 10, 16, 17, 28, 29, 30
February	25, 26
March	4, 5, 11, 12, 13, 14, 25, 31

April	1, 7, 8, 9, 20, 21, 27, 28, 29
May	5, 6, 18, 19, 25, 26
June	1, 2, 14, 15, 21, 22, 28, 29, 30
July	11, 12, 13, 18, 19, 20, 26, 27
August	8, 9, 15, 16, 22, 23
September	4, 5, 11, 12, 18, 19, 20
October	1, 2, 8, 9, 10, 16, 17, 29, 30
November	4, 5, 6, 12, 13, 25, 26
December	2, 3, 9, 10, 11, 23, 24, 29, 30

Cutting nails

January	11, 12, 13, 14, 15, 18, 19, 20, 21
February	7, 8, 9, 10, 11, 14, 16
March	6, 8, 9, 10, 14, 15
April	2, 3, 5, 6
May	4, 7, 8, 9, 10, 11, 27, 28, 29, 30, 31
June	3, 4, 5, 6, 7, 23, 25, 26, 27
July	1, 2, 3, 21, 22, 23, 24, 25, 28, 29, 30, 31
August	17, 19, 20, 24, 25, 26
September	13, 16, 17, 21, 22, 23, 24
October	11, 13, 15, 18, 19, 20, 21, 22
November	15, 16, 17, 18

December   4, 5, 6, 7, 8

Therapies, massage and self-pampering

January	1, 2, 8, 9, 10, 16, 17, 28, 29, 30
February	5, 6, 12, 13, 25, 26
March	4, 5, 11, 12, 13, 24, 25, 31
April	1, 7, 8, 9, 20, 21, 27, 28, 29
May	5, 6, 18, 19, 25, 26
June	1, 2, 14, 15, 21, 22, 28, 29, 30
July	11, 12, 13, 18, 19, 20, 26, 27
August	8, 9, 15, 16, 22, 23
September	4, 5, 11, 12, 18, 19, 20
October	1, 2, 8, 9, 10, 16, 17, 29, 30
November	4, 5, 6, 12, 13, 25, 26
December	2, 3, 9, 10, 11, 23, 24, 29, 30